GETTING EVEN

The Equalizing Law of Relationship

Philip Lichtenberg

UNIVERSITY
PRESS OF
AMERICA

For my sons,
Erik, Andrew, Thomas and Peter.

Their creativity and caring
nourish my hope for a decent society.

ACKNOWLEDGEMENTS

In addition to acknowledgements in the text, I want to add my appreciation to a few of the many who helped me continue and complete this project.

To the late Professor George Stern, to Dr. L. Diane Bernard and to Professor Michael Krausz for their support and encouragement.

To Alice Matusow and Professor Ann Berthoff for many helpful editorial suggestions.

To my wife, Elsa, for her constant challenge, support and patience.

To the students in the Graduate School of Social Work and Social Research of Bryn Mawr College, for whom these essays were originally written, and who pushed me to continue with them and to bring them to the light of day.

To Lorraine Wright who typed many of the early versions of these essays.

I have freely used quotations in the text, often of extended passages, and I gratefully acknowledge the following:

"On Being Thoroughly Alive" is reprinted with slight modification, from *Et cetera,* Volume 37, No. 3, by permission of the International Society for General Semantics.

To Henry Holt and Company, Inc. for permission to use quotations from *I Never Promised You a Rose Garden* by Hannah Green and from *The Freudian Wish and Its Place in Ethics* by Edwin B. Holt.

To the American Medical Association for permission to quote from "Time Perspective and Intimacy: Their Effect on Patient Behavior in Occupational Therapy," which appeared in the *A.M.A. Archives of General Psychiatry,* 1959, Volume 1, pages 425–433, Copyright 1959 American Medical Association.

For an excerpt from Conrad Aiken's "Your Obituary, Well Written" reprinted by permission of Schocken Books, Inc. from *The Collected Short Stories of Conrad Aiken* by Conrad Aiken, Copyright © 1922–25, 1927–35, 1941, 1950, 1952, 1953, 1955–62, 1964 by Conrad Aiken.

To McGraw-Hill Book Company for permission to use quotations from "Institutional Social Education of Severely Maladjusted Girls," by Asger Hansen which appeared in *International Trends in Mental Health,* Henry P. David, Editor.

CONTENTS

CHAPTER 1

INTRODUCTION

The essays in this book tie together the most serious distortions in the ways we create and experience our lives in every day activity and the most pronounced failings of society as we inhabit it and as we make it function. In these writings as well, I explore connections that I believe exist between the highest moments of personal experience and what I consider to be ideal and effective operations of our social institutions. The worst and the best of our lives, taken individually and collectively, constitute the framework of my interest in these writings.

Some of the ideas presented here come directly from my work with people who are admittedly suffering. Many of the case histories and the examples cited in the text concern people who are emotionally disturbed, persons who are on the public welfare rolls, who are considered to be juvenile delinquents, or who belong to various segments of the underclasses of our social order. These troubled and troubling individuals often have lived within institutions which are organized expressly to care for them and to provide some kind of useful social service to them, and yet, when I looked not at the unhappy individuals but also at the organizations that were supposed to serve for them, I saw troubles in the institutions comparable to those in the individuals they were to nurture. The routines of these institutions were invariably unpalatable as a consequence of the limitations imposed upon them by the misgivings, mean-spiritedness and faulty practices of the larger social system. It became important to me to attend simultaneously to the problems of the persons and the disorders of the social institutions, as I hope it will be significant to my reader as well.

Thus, while the ideas in these essays began as part of an attempt to understand the difficulties encountered by these hurting individuals and to develop methods for alleviating their hurts and their handicaps, I came to appreciate that adequate understanding of seriously disturbed persons entails basic social criticism. The treatment accorded suffering individuals in our society is abominable. Mental hospitals are far from what we know how to offer if we use established knowledge and apply ourselves in an enlightened way, and we have become increasingly grudging even in the use of such hospitals. Public welfare is degrading and, by now, itself degraded. Prisons, no longer even pretending to be rehabilitative, are inhumane. The homeless are treated ineptly and the poor, an ever increasing proportion of our population, are subjected to unnecessary abuse and pain.

When we lift up our eyes from the victims and peer into the conditions of the institutions that serve the worst off in society, we seldom examine closely and critically what life is like in these settings for the helpers as well as the receivers, the staff as well as the clients, those who administer the institutions as well as those who are affected by them. If things are bad for patients, clients, delinquents and inmates, they are also difficult and unrewarding for therapists, caseworkers, police officers and prison guards. It is hard to find a human service institution with high morale these days, and even the best of them reflect great frustration and sense of defeat when people compare the purposes and goals of the institution to what actually occurs. When one of us is a client, she thinks her helper is well off; however, when she assumes the position of helper, she is forced to acknowledge the constraints, the pressures, the isolation, the lack of support that is available to her, and she too becomes deeply dissatisfied.

And if, after expanding our field of vision to include all members of helping organizations, doctors and nurses as well as patients, and receptionists and administrators too, we can take the next step and look around at other institutions and at the citizenry at large, a further realization comes upon us. We need to move beyond human service institutions precisely because in studying them closely we see vividly that they are not unique. We are all suffering and the way we are organized socially is not serving our common needs. The lessons in the lives of the most unhappy, I intend to show, touch the fears, social binds and struggles that we have all experienced in every institution that touches our lives, from schools for our children to government presumably under our control.

When we acknowledge that we are all hurting, and hurting more than it is conventionally proper to reveal, or more than we permit ourselves even to experience, we can easily fall into feeling our victimhood and in doing so increase our despair. Yet no one is totally victim. Each social structure in which we participate in our daily lives is the creative result of our actions and of those who participate within or around that structure. Every institution is shaped by the weak as well as the strong, by the latecomer as by the initiator, by the casual visitor as by the manager. Whether one person contributes as much as the next in the construction, reconstruction and day-by-day reaffirmation of the institution, each and every individual adds her share or his to the organization, develops habits for living within it, and invests herself to some degree in its maintenance and development. These habits are among the ways in which we all engage in self-contradictions, for we often defend that which gives us little and costs us dear.

If it is true, as I believe, (and as Freud has maintained so eloquently), that each person has in some respects erected the structures around him to serve or protect him, then it is also true that the impetus to change social institutions raises real threats to all members of the community, not only the ruling class or privileged people, as some assert. Each individual is threatened with the removal during social reconstruction of paintakingly created defenses against everyday injustice, exploitation and autocratic rule. Any promise of enriched human existence is necessarily accompanied by the fear that worse structures will arise on the remains of the old ones, not simply because there are villains waiting for their chance to control even more of the world, but also because we who make the institutions, all of us, will be afraid for ourselves and will institute safety devices and insurance procedures that will become structuralized and limiting in their new way. We are all responsible for what exists now and we will all be responsible for deciding whether we will change the institutions in which we live and work.

I am not saying that we hope to become the makers of our history in some future time. We are right now creating and inventing that future, and we do well to remember always that fact.

The essential social critique that I will follow in these essays can be stated in very simple form: authoritarian forms of social relations by their inherent nature produce, encourage and sustain conflict-ridden and weakly gratifying lives; true vitality can only come about from instituting equalitarianism into social interchange. Vitality, productivity and equalitarianism go together, and discordant living and authoritarianism are interconnected. Thus, I will argue that we find mature liveliness in solving life's problems within equalitarian social relations or in striving to modify authoritarian institutions into equalitarian ones; and we find in authoritarian forms of social relations the opposites of vitality, deadness and agitation, usually in combination such that deadness is followed by agitation which in turn is succeeded by new deadness. While equalitarianism promotes liveliness, authoritarianism fosters either lifelessness or conflict-ridden behavior.

To pursue the idea that equalitarianism fosters intense liveliness, I will look at what it means to be truly alive, vitally involved in daily existence. Because we are all complex persons, moved by diverse needs, and impulses from within, and also caught in many demands and stimulations from the world around us, our actions associated with true aliveness must give inclusive and harmonious form to a good part of all these forces. When we are vital in our actions, we are inventing efficient and incorporative patterns of operation. We are quickened and animated as individuals to the degree that we are fully and complexly unified, integrated within ourselves at the same time that we are integrated within groups and collectivities around us.

There are two contrasts to such vitality in life, not one. The first opposite is deadness, estrangement, apathy, bare existence; the second is agitation, and excitement that constitutes high arousal when many desires and stimuli intermix in abrasive or contradictory ways. If vitality involves integrated fullness, then one of its negations is emptiness. We find our lives empty when we narrowly restrict the forces we allow to control our behavior at any moment. We try to compartmentalize our actions rather than enrich them, and our penalty for the attempted simplification is that we close ourselves off from the richness of life, yield instead to a kind of deadness or anti-life.

Because few of us choose to persist always as barely alive, we invariably try to make our actions more complex. We overcome our own restrictiveness. Yet not all complexity is productive of vitality. An individual can respond to many desires and many external cues at one instant but lack the capacity to coordinate these internal and external forces into productive action. Such a person may be very much aroused, but not fully alive because the desires and stimuli stand in opposition to each other. The fulfillment of one need may bring about the frustration of a different one, as when a person wishes to grant full independence to a lover and never be threatened with jealous feelings, or the expression of a desire may violate the wishes of other people in the field of action. The sum total of satisfaction is quite low as a result.

The conception of equalitarianism and authoritarianism developed in these essays asserts that in all human transactions there are negotiations among the participants such that the persons involved in fact end up with approximately equal amounts of gratification. Whether concrete relations between persons are characterized as equalitarian or authoritarian, they always tend to produce equality of fulfillment. This is a strong position to take, one that is usually hard to accept because it violates common sense or the received view of things, but I hold to it quite firmly.

I first came upon this position quite by accident. I was at the beginning of my professional career, engaged in carrying out an experiment originally designed by the psychologist Henry A. Murray and the physicist Percy Bridgman, an experiment to be used with Harvard undergraduates who were being intensively studied. I did a small pilot study with a young woman friend of mine and her mother. First, I asked the two women to outline a plot for a play. After they had completed this first step, I asked them to talk with each other and create one new plot that incorporated material from their individual attempts. I tape recorded and transcribed this joint plot and was, therefore, able to compare what was in each individual plot and what ended up being included in the joint plot.

Simply listening to the two women on the tape led to the conclusion that the mother had entered a great deal of her material into the final product and the daughter relatively little. The mother had dominated, or so it seemed, and a simple count of items from the two plots should confirm the difference noted impressionistically. The long and short of the matter, however, is that a count of separate items from the two women in the collective plot was almost exactly equal. What had seemed to be a great disparity between their contributions was not present. They had equalized in their negotiating process.

The experiment was then applied to the Harvard students. A group of them had been asked to write sermons to the world. It was posed that this was their last day on earth and that the world's population was awaiting their advice. From each sermon I took four salient points. I then called in the students in pairs. To each member of the pair, one of my associates instructed that the student was to convince another person of the four points he had developed. These were wonderful points, we asserted, and we wanted the student to persuade a colleague of them. When the two students had been individually instructed, they were brought together in a room with lights, movie cameras, tape recorders and instructed anew. This time they were told together that they had eleven minutes to create the five best ideas to give to the world.

Pairs of students followed different strategies in combining these two sets of instructions. Some found a way to include all eight individual points in the five final ideas. Others fought to have their individual points included and ended with two from each student, or possibly three to two. In all six pairs, however, an equalizing tendency appeared, as it had in the pilot study with the young woman and her mother.

I came to believe that all transactions involve this equalizing tendency and that close inspection of the sadist and the masochist, the child and the parent, the boss and the worker, lovers, and others in all kinds of work and play reveals over and over that what may appear unequal is instead and in fact mutual. The negotiations that take place within human relations, the support and resistance, directness and circumlocution, asking and compromising, determine not the equality of gratification but the *amount* of satisfaction that is produced by the social intercourse. If one person tries to take more from an interaction with his collaborators, that individual invariably induces counteractions from others in the direction of equalization. Since the counteractions diminish the achievements possible for the transaction, the attempted aggrandizement leads to a lower level of gratification for all involved. If a person tries to sacrifice himself in the interests of someone else — if, for instance, a father denies himself to provide for some requests made by his child, — that person similarly stimulates corrective trends in the others such that lesser amounts of fulfillment are shared in an equalizing way. The child does not simply gain from his father's sacrifice; he becomes aware too of the father's self-inflicted loss and is confused by the win-lose nature of the relationship. Try as he might to disguise his sacrifice, the father communicates his self-denial and his son, at some level, responds to it. When a person implements intentions toward equal accomplishments and enrichments, on the other hand, he activates forces that facilitate high levels of satisfaction because every participant is made to feel that her needs or his matter.

Since people differ in their needs and abilities, they take different benefits from a transaction. Accordingly, when I speak of equalized amounts of satisfaction, I am not referring to the same or identical satisfactions. The infant and her parent equalize in their relationship, but when they equalize, they derive different advantages from the relation. One of the basic images of pleasure described in the psychological literature, a favorite image in my own mind, may illustrate the point: an infant in deep bond with a willing mother while nursing at the mother's breast. Both child and mother derive vast quantities of joy and enrichment in the ideal nursing situation, but the particular pleasures they derive are significantly different from each other. The child's delight in the warmth of the breast and the milk is paired with the mother's pleasure in having her body stimulated, her laden breast emptied, her infant responsive to her nurturing behavior. Such equality between people, then, does not depend upon sameness of competence or need, nor does it represent identity in the structure of the pleasures experienced. It means personal equality in the sense of equality of gratification of the person as a whole.[1]

If all human relationships entail such equalizing tendencies, what then distinguishes equalitarianism from authoritarianism? After all,

5

there is negotiation and equilibration in authoritarian as well as equalitarian forms of social association, and I am here asserting that approximate equality occurs in either circumstance. At least part of the distinction between equalitarianism and authoritarianism comes down to the following: equalitarianism involves the conduct of every day life according to the assumption that all relations equilibrate toward personally equal amounts of satisfaction, whereas authoritarianism proceeds through behavior based on the assumption that inequality is the probable outcome of transactions. One fact is that some kind of equality is always the result of transactions; but another fact is that some people act as if this were true, and thus behave in an equalitarian manner, while other people act as if it were not true, and thereby implement authoritarianism.

There is a second distinction between equalitarianism and authoritarianism. In all human encounters there is division of the effort, with each person responsible for her own side of the transaction; consequently, these separate efforts must be coordinated if goals and satisfaction and sharing of rewards are to be achieved. In all human relations there is authority. "Authority is basic to social relationship. It organizes individuals to each other with respect to their needs individually and their concerns as a group"[2] From this perspective, authority is any influence that refers simultaneously to self-assertion and to coordination among persons interacting with each other. Authority is influence that enables individual definition and group articulation to take place concurrently. All of the negotiations and equilibrations between people that inevitably lead toward equality constitute authority. Whatever ties are created among people develop from some form of authority; it is the nature of authority that varies.

Since all social transactions require authority, it is important to determine what distinguishes authoritarianism from equalitarianism in this domain. The question is frequently posed as, "What is the difference between being authoritarian and being authoritative?" Since all human relationships need the bonding action of authority to move forward, authoritarian relations are not simply those in which authority is present and equalitarian relations are not simply those without authority. Because authoritarianism is based upon assumptions about inherent inequality and scarcity of gratifications, authoritarian authority centers upon gathering and securing the authority's own satisfactions or protecting his interests in an exploitative world. Conversely, because equalitarianism involves assumptions of mutual inclusiveness and reciprocity in gains, equalitarian authority is used in the interests of maximum goal achievements. Authority tied to exclusivity of outcomes is authoritarian; authority aimed at inclusive sharing of satisfactions is equalitarian.

In both equalitarian and authoritarian relationships there is equalization and there is authority. The differences between equalitarian and authoritarian relations stem from the diverse assumptions that underlie behavior and determine its qualities. An equalitarian approach to life assumes the possibility of reaching high levels of pleasure, whereas an authoritarian approach aims at securing or insuring whatever gains can be taken from the situation. Within an equalitarian framework, much open sharing of information and active decision-making are esteemed; within an authoritarian framework, the already known and the least threatening cues to behavior are most prized. The goal of the following essays is to demonstrate how these differences surface and affect private and social life.

These are studies in psychological thought and in social thought. I have tried to avoid psychologizing social life, wanting not to reduce matters that are of social and political import to terms of character and attitude, because I am clear in my mind that major social changes are coming and need to be informed by all levels of understanding. It is too easy to become caught up in the intricacies of psychological life divorced from social struggle and to lose one's way as a contributor to social change. Moreover, I have steered clear of that social thought which debases the personal, which dehumanizes people in the name of social reform and social revolution. Any correction of society that fails to assimilate the highest wisdom of personality theory seems to me doomed to be unnecessarily destructive of human life. Too much psychologizing and too little are both harmful to our labors; too much and too little politicizing cause the same damage. For real changes to take place, change that moves the individual and the society, we need both ingredients in appropriate measures.

Notes

1. This is excellently argued in John Macmurray's *The Clue to History*. New York: Harper. 1939.
2. Ellen Wood Freeman. *The Use of Authority.* Unpublished M.S.S. Paper. Bryn Mawr, Pennsylvania, 19010: Bryn Mawr College Canaday Library, 1973.

CHAPTER 2

CASE REPORT: A FLICKER OF LIFE[1]

There was a moment in my professional life when I became aware of a simple equation which gave life, or at least a flicker of life, to a woman who had been dead to reality. It was a passing moment, dramatic in its effects upon all the participants, a reminder that the daily activities of workers in mental health have great potential, yet significant precisely because it was set off from the usual run of things. In many ways that encounter was a central motive force behind these essays, morally because it posed a delicate problem for me, emotionally because it was vivid in its impact, and intellectually because it demonstrated graphically the differences between authoritarian and equalitarian leadership.

The setting was the library of a small state hospital which also served as a conference room. It was not a large room, and with a group of people seated around the table there was little space for free movement except for a small area just inside the entrance door. A number of us on the staff were gathered for our weekly case conference, whose purpose was to offer a diagnosis and treatment plan for patients recently admitted to the hospital. The conference also had the purpose of teaching young psychiatrists in training how to construct a diagnosis and decide which kinds of treatment should be prescribed.

The director of the hospital, a forty-five-year-old psychiatrist, was responsible for directing the conference. He had a generally quiet and permissive demeanor with both his patients and his students. He was intelligent but less scholarly than he aspired to be. The associate director was a psychiatrist whose dealings with psychotic people were inconsistent, sometimes insightful and wonderful, sometimes downright terrible. There were five physicians in their first year of residency. Enamored of the subtleties of psychiatry, they were an intellectualized and rather cold group, more concerned with ideas in the abstract than with developing ways to working closely with disturbed people. Also in the room that day was a young clinical psychologist, gifted as a clinician, especially with certain types of patients, with high scientific ambitions and continually unhappy mien. One of my colleagues in research and I rounded out the staff.

The patient was ushered into the library by an attendant, greeted by the director, and seated at the head of the table between the director and the door. She was a brilliant, ugly, quick, intense and mad woman, fifty-seven years of age, who had spent a considerable portion of her past twenty-five years in various state hospitals. She was the center of attention today as she had been many times before in several hospitals, with different directors, audiences and interrogators surrounding her. This particular episode began with the director asking her to talk about her problems in living. For the next five minutes she gave a reasonably coherent account of how Dr. M. had advised her to do such and such, while her husband had suggested a second course and her friend had proposed a third alternative; we later discovered that the elements in her story had preceded her first hospital admission twenty-five years earlier. She was generally organized in telling the story, but there was a tone of growing excitement in her recitation.

Suddenly she rose from her chair, rapidly strode the five paces open to her, behind the director and away from the door, came back to her seat, and then moved wildly to and fro. She was breathing rapidly, speaking wildly, almost shrieking, and there was little sense in the words she spoke. She was, in the vernacular, acting crazy. After allowing two minutes or so of this display to continue, with each remark and each pace of the patient growing more excited than the previous one, the director went to the door, called the attendant, and had the woman returned to her room.

Some of us were quite upset by what we had witnessed. Arguing from some of our pretheoretical notions, we claimed that we, the staff, had turned the woman crazy before our eyes by our manner and our behavior. We said, rather forcefully, as I recall, that this woman could be met in the same circumstance without going beserk; as a matter of fact, we said, we could do it right here and now. To our surprise, the director picked up our challenge. We were given a few minutes to prepare while the others had coffee, and arrangements were made for the woman to be brought back to the library for a second conference.

We laid plans for the clinical psychologist to implement. He was to establish three elements in the unfolding of the interview: he would be *reactive* in his relationship with her; he would *support* those efforts on her part that promoted the development of a productive analysis of her problem; and he would *disallow or deny* actions that were distracting to the work of diagnosis.

He was to be reactive — that is, to let the patient set the pace, choose the direction of the conversation, give color to the episode, and so forth — simply because in this type of emotional disturbance, which we were diagnosing as manic-depressive psychosis, the patient must feel responsible for the outcome of any experience. Our prescription was derived from the analysis that the crazy behavior of this woman was manic excitement. Although manic persons need to feel responsible for the work they undertake, they are self-defeating. They try to correct their self-defeating behavior by having steering devices outside themselves, beyond their control, but they deteriorate in any scene in which they do not have these outside corrective devices, or in which these are ineffective or untrustworthy. Therefore, it would be sufficient for the psychologist to note that the patient had gotten herself hospitalized by her own behavior, and now they were both subject to the policies and practices of the hospital. He would indicate to her that she must lead the way, since it was her life under study, and he would try to follow her initiatives.

That it was not enough for him to be only non-directive should be clear from my account of the first session. The director of the hospital had been passive, though very attentive; yet his passivity had had the effect, after the opening minutes, of inducing the madness. We felt that the patient's bizarre demonstration was a signal from her — a signal to indicate that the situation was either incomprehensible or bothersome to her. Our failure to respond to this signal was a major error.

As we saw it, the determining factor in relating to this woman was for the interviewer to be reactive, not merely passive. The ground for establishing this difference lay in the task to which both the woman and the psychologist were addressing themselves. Although they were in different positions, they shared the common task of understanding the nature of the problem that had brought her to the hospital and that continued to plague her. Passivity in the relationship meant to be following the woman without taking into account the *raison d'etre* of the relationship; reactivity, on the other hand, recognized the need to be responsive both to the woman and to the purpose of the relationship, the task, mediating between them when discrepancies or interferences arose. Thus, the psychologist was to support productive efforts on her part and deny tangential actions. He would be non-directive when she was speaking directly to issues pertinent to diagnosis, that is, to their common effort, and directive or corrective when she was off the mark, digressing erratically as manic persons are wont to do.

Within a few minutes, the staff members and students returned from coffee and the patient was recalled. Now the second diagnostic conversation within the hour began. The psychologist explained to the woman that they were to work together so that a diagnosis could be made and appropriate treatment prescribed. He went on to say that he understood that the necessity for the diagnosis and treatment resulted from her prior, socially incomprehensible actions that had brought about her hospitalization. He prepared her to recognize that he would suggest certain topics during the course of the conversation in order for the task of diagnosis to be completed, and he would interrupt her on occasion when he felt this would expedite their work. He then reiterated the question with which the director had begun the first interview — would she tell us about her problems in living? After she had told her tale briefly, the psychologist observed that she had mentioned Dr. M. and he would like to know who this doctor was. He was, surprisingly, the physician who had committed her many years previously, whom she had not seen in some time, though she had been speaking about him as if her contact with him had been recent.

The psychologist asked about her husband and others to whom she had referred in her account. She was allowed a few comments on each of these people, but when he had gathered significant information, yet before irrelevancies had seeped in, the psychologist informed her that he possessed sufficient material on the particular topic she was describing. Once or twice the woman tried to pursue a matter after the psychologist had indicated she should stop. With gentle and firm insistence, the psychologist informed her that he was sure she was about to say something that was interesting, but that it was not to the point of the immediate discussion. If they were to finish their work, they must keep an even course and not be distracted. This tactic continued for the next half hour, a thirty minutes that passed more quickly, and even more dramatically, than the initial seven-minutes interview.

During this period a truly astounding change occurred in the woman. In place of an ugly, misshapen, wild and hideous figure appeared a woman of exceptional depth, warmth and sensitivity. She began to recall her father and mother with extreme clarity, though she had not seen them for years. The cruelty of her father, a wealthy man, who wanted a son not a daughter, was relived before us in a description that can be characterized only as elegant in its style and its perceptiveness. Her marriage to an alcoholic man, in a desperate bid to free herself from her family, the burden that this new relation became, and the eventual dissolution of her marriage, all came out in clear, reasonable and insightful narrative.

This discourse was not without its bitter taste, however, since it would be foolish to believe that craziness is only an escape from unhappy memories. Accompanying her reconstruction was a thick, enveloping and overpowering anxiety. It was as if she contained the whole feeling of panic while sitting and conversing, as if the feelings of a hundred anxious episodes were collected and concentrated into a single point of time. The experiencing of this profound and unsettling anxiety could be permitted by the woman only when she could trust that a partner was available who would prevent her from destroying herself in the midst of such agony. She had seldom until that moment found such a partner, and so she had substituted the crazy behavior for the sensible thoughts and unbearable feelings.

When sufficient information was gathered and the patient had begun to feel fatigue from her exertion, she was taken back to her room. This had been a fragment in her life when the depths of her complex character had been activated and organized in a complete way. It was a unique opportunity for her, one that she was seldom to see again so far as I have been able to know of her.

The patient's experience was not the only one that changed from the first to the second session; the rest of us in that room went through the same emotional journey. In the opening encounter, when the patient jumped up and walked and shouted widly, we became tremendously uneasy and unsettled. It is a scary business to be with someone who is at the heights of craziness, no matter how long one has been around disturbed persons. We were infected with her agitation. We looked nervously at each other, we laughed anxiously when she said something funny, and we rapidly ended the episode by calling the attendant and having her returned to her room. In her later experience with the psychologist, she brought us to a whole new realm of pleasure and understanding.

The two separate sessions with the patient were also characterized by major differences in authority. The main burden of the criticism made after the first encounter with the patient was that the director had not used his position wisely; and the change introduced by the psychologist in the second encounter represented a revised expression of authority. If we accept the fact that authority is a means to the positive coordination of separate persons as they work to define and reach common goals, then it is a means to control faulty efforts of uniting self and others as well. The director of the hospital was *laissez-faire* in his authority and the psychologist was equalitarian, so that we observed a contrast between authoritarian and equalitarian forms of authority.

The director asserted the *laissez-faire* mode of authoritarianism in the following way. He clearly occupied the post of highest recognized authority by his role in training the psychiatric residents, his granting permission for researchers to sit at the conference table, and by his leadership in the conduct of the first interview. But he did little more than to occupy that position, initiate and then terminate the interview, and open the floor for discussion by the professional persons who remained when the woman left the room. He did not connect the patient with the other persons in the room to the point that they became partners associated with a common task; and he did not keep the patient and himself firmly to the purpose of the transaction.

The authority he used, while permissive and passive, was self-enhancing and demeaning of others at one and the same time because it was disconnected from the collective function which was its origin. Persons become leaders because they are effective in bringing successful social achievements to fruition. When they accept the position of central influence without attending to the inherent requirements of the joint endeavor, they act as if the power given to them is a sign of personal worth and superiority. *Laissez-faire* forms of authority systematically emphasize the individuality of the leader and obscure or diminish the others who are also part of the social transaction.

We were fortunate that the director's authoritarianism was of the *laissez-faire* type. Had he been dominatingly authoritarian, had he been directive and overly assertive of himself, he would have inhibited any challenge to the way he conducted the session and he would have disallowed any alternative effort like that carried out by the psychologist. We were grateful that he permitted such an experiment, and we were impressed with his courage and stature in risking a comparison in which he might come out second.

The psychologist, lacking all the concomitant powers that the director had by virtue of his place in the institution, brought into play effective authority by taking into account the special characteristics of the patient, the roles of the various professionals and the nature of the task for which the conference was called. He saw himself as both directed and constrained by these separate forces, as well as a mediator among them. He was immersed in the group, caught up by the patient's story, attentive to the requirement that a diagnosis be established, and respectful of each individual present.

The two interviews with the patient contained both contrasting qualities of vitality in life and different patterns of authority. From a life that had alternated between numbness and excitement, this woman for a brief moment knew what it is like to live in interaction with others. For her it was an interlude, perhaps in the long run an unwelcome one since it revealed a possibility that was probably not to be renewed. Herein is the moral issue of whether we had the right to raise her hopes by creating a moment of vital living and then not following through with more such encounters. Yet for the rest of us the simple experiment was instructive. Between confused, agitated existence and life with integrated fullness there is perhaps a shorter distance than our current understandings permit us to see.

Notes

1. This is a modified presentation of an article of the same name published in the *Pennsylvania Psychiatric Quarterly,* 1966, Volume 6.

CHAPTER 3

ON BEING THOROUGHLY ALIVE[1]

It is common to all of us that we experience many lives, from bare existence to utmost vitality. We differ in how often we feel truly alive, and we distinguish ourselves from each other by the details and circumstances that allow us to reach thorough aliveness. The case conference in the previous chapter in which patient and staff shifted dramatically between uneasiness and confidence, manic excitement and strikingly deep aliveness, illustrates this range along the scale of vitality and animation.

In his book on synonyms and antonyms, Fernald provides a concise statement of this dimension.

"*Alive* applies to all degrees of life, from that which shows one to be barely *existing* or *existed* as a living thing, as when we say that he is just *alive*, to that which implies the very utmost of vitality and power, as in the words 'he is all *alive*,' 'thoroughly *alive*.'"[2]

Examples of both bare existence and thorough aliveness come up again and again. Yet, while we all probably have experienced thorough aliveness, we do not know sufficiently well its basic ingredients nor do we know how to create it when we wish. It would be helpful and promising if we did understand these conditions because we might then be able to develop more such times. This kind of understanding is especially important in measuring the differences between equalitarian and authoritarian organizations.

To understand the components of thorough aliveness, we can abstract four characteristics that must be present. These are illustrated by examples taken sometimes from my clinical and research practice, sometimes from technical literature, and sometimes from a contemporary novel about mental illness and its effects. Each characteristic is important in its own right, but all must be integrated to create the experience of vitality.

Thorough aliveness is characterized by a special consciousness.

When we are thoroughly alive, our awareness or conscious experience is marked by richness, vividness and fullness. There is an oceanic aspect of consciousness, a total, uniform at-oneness which we associate with complete embeddedness in living. We feel full of our consciousness, yet not overpowered by it. Things appear to be just right, not too much and not too little, fulfilling and integrating to us as whole persons. We can call this feeling awe, contentment, or ecstasy, and we can define it as religious, sexual, or athletic, but what we find in our consciousness is a positive and global experiencing.

Abraham Maslow describes this consciousness in his discussion of what he calls "peak experiences:"

> "the object tends to be seen as a whole, as a complete unit, detached from relations, from possible usefulness, from expediency...."
>
> "a self-justifying moment which carries its own intrinsic value with it."
>
> "a special flavor of wonder, of awe, of reverence...."
>
> "relatively ego-transcending, self-forgetful, egoless."[3]

Because the consciousness that pervades thorough aliveness is so positive and appealing, we must be especially careful to recognize that becoming thoroughly alive does not always take place in benign or healthy contexts. It may be the one positive moment within a series of struggles and disagreements, the resolution of differences, for example, or the coming together of people even as they experience adversity. As the following example demostrates, this special consciousness can develop in contexts which few of us would consider happy.

Example 1. In the novel, *I Never Promised You a Rose Garden*, Hannah Green relates the following scene. The heroine, Deborah Blau, is on Ward D, a ward for disturbed, destructive or deteriorated mental patients. Her friend, Carla, had moved out to Ward B, a sign that her mental condition had improved; but now, in a regression, she is being returned to Ward D to the accompaniment of secret giggles by the student nurses, giggles which offend Deborah:

> "They had not been talking about some nut, but about Carla, a Carla who was good all the way to the bone; good enough even to be kind when Deborah had struck her at the core of her pain.
>
> "No one, seeing Deborah and Carla, would have known that they were friends. It would be an imposition, incomprehensible to the sane, for Deborah to greet Carla, who was in distress and who would be sorry later if a greeting drove her to violence or even rudeness. Deborah did not look at Carla; she only waited behind her stone mask until she would see the secret sign from Carla that meant recognition.
>
> "When the sign was given, they moved toward each other appearing as elaborately unconcerned as they could. Deborah smiled very slightly, but then a strange thing happened. Into the flat, gray, blurred, and two-dimensional waste of her vision, Carla came three-dimensionally and in color, as a whole and real as a mouthful of hot coffee or coming-to in a pack.
>
> "'Hi,' Deborah said, on a barely rising tone.
>
> "'Hi.'"[4]

Deborah's experience is similar to that which often occurs when people acquire eyeglasses. As soon as they put the glasses on, the world becomes more sharply focused, the colors jump out to reach them, and they say that they have a new sense of the world around them. This does not take place in some spectacular event and it is not always obvious to others that the transformation has taken place.

Sometimes we can become fully alive in harsh circumstances and others may never really know that anything out of the ordinary has happened unless we choose to share our perceptions.

Thourough aliveness is characterized by coherently organized expression of many forces within the personality system.

For a person to become thoroughly alive, both the desires that motivate him and the stimuli that impinge upon him from the environment must be allowed free play in his psyche. To be alert and aroused means risking complexity of experience. To open oneself to the chaos of the inner life and the diversity of forces always active in the immediate world means that ideas and impulses that have been put away because they seemed dangerous may have to be tapped again. Needs that were dormant, because they were satisfied and receded or because they were unsatisfied and repressed, take on new demanding qualities this time, in this world, at this juncture of life's possibilities.

When many desires and stimuli are mobilized in the mind, they may become organized in a coordinated system and lead to full gratification. But they may also be too much for the individual to master. They may rise up within him and be brought together in a disjointed, antagonistic form. Rather than experiencing thorough aliveness, the person may be torn apart by the unintegrated forces that have been unleashed. The person is overstimulated and, like a child too aroused at bedtime, cannot put things together and quiet down.

When a person is able to bring much of herself into her dealings with others without internal contradictions, she feels full within herself and at one with the world. From this rising up of many thoughts and emotions within the person and the functional, successful and unimpeded flow of desires between the person and others comes a sense of the completeness of the experience. Any time that person can coherently organize much of herself in a productive interchange with others, she will feel very much alive.

One can be highly aroused, very much excited, however, without being thoroughly alive, as evidenced by the fact that people are ingesting drugs, gambling, fornicating, struggling for fame, waging war, playing football and engaging otherwise in intense activities which they hope will dispel their malaise. People drink alcohol or gamble as a means of raising the level of psychological activity within themselves. Drinking temporarily lowers inhibitions and permits repressed needs access to consciousness or behavior. Gambling induces the person to attend closely to details and probabilities in his situational world. At its extreme, such excitement is registered as agitation; at lesser levels, it can be irritability, tension, mock gaiety or abrasive sensationalism. When the lover tries too much to be aroused, he becomes excited but not thoroughly alive. Although excitement may pervade the whole of one's sensitivities as a manifestation of much astir within, in agitation one is not only aroused but also assailed by internal dissonance.

Early in his writings, Freud delineates these differences in high levels of psychological tension:

"Our speech, the outcome of the experience of many generations, distinguishes with admirable delicacy between those forms and degrees of heightening of excitation which are still useful for mental activity.... because they raise the free energy of all cerebral functions uniformly, and those forms and degrees which restrict that activity because they partly increase and partly inhibit these psychical functions in a manner that is *not* uniform. The first are given the name of 'incitement,' and the second, 'excitement.'* An interesting conversation, or a cup of tea or coffee has an 'inciting' [stimulating] effect; a dispute or a considerable dose of alcohol has an 'exciting' one. While incitement only arouses the urge to employ the increased excitation functionally, excitement seeks to discharge itself in more or less violent ways which are almost or even actually pathological.

*[In German, *'Anregung'* = 'incitement,' 'stimulation'; *'Aufregung'* = 'excitement,' 'agitation.']"[5]

The woman in "Flicker of Life" expressed excitement in her manic behavior because she was unable to organize herself around a task and because others could not provide the social and material supports that would enable her to behave in a unified manner. She subsequently came alive when the psychologist helped her to integrate her actions. Both incitement and excitement represent the mobilization and interplay of many desires and stimuli, but incitement (full aliveness) represents non-contradictory integration of these forces, while excitement derives from the contradictoriness among the set of forces that are straining within the whole.

My second example, also from experience in a mental hospital, illustrates this shift from agitation under one set of circumstances to preoccupied, coherent, life-meaning engagement when the proper conditions are present.

Example 2. Some years ago I led a continuing, informal discussion group concerned with those ideas in the theory of small groups that could be useful to occupational therapists. We talked about group projects in occupational therapy, work and play. We also studied directly individuals at work in occupational therapy settings. As a consequence of our collaboration, we became highly sensitive to episodes in which everything fell into place, coordinated and fulfilling. The following case description is from a report on one aspect of our work in the seminars.

"Mrs. A., aged twenty-one, a white woman, first manifested bizarre behavior three days before she was admitted to our hospital. The demands made upon her by her marriage and the loss of emotional support of her parents were felt to be the precipitating causes of her illness. In the early days of her hospitalization the patient was hyperactive, provocative, and seductive. Gradually her behavior changed, until she appeared somewhat depressed at the end of her three months in the hospital.

"The patient spent a considerable amount of time in occupational therapy engaged in frantic activities. She tended to do everything at once, trying to talk, drink coffee, and work on projects. She spent much of her time knitting simple, quickly-completed items for herself. On a typical day during her first month of hospitalization she would knit for a short period, play pool, knit again, play the piano, socialize with the male patients, and then repeat the cycle. Concurrently she would talk, sing, chew gum, and smoke. When occupational therapy sessions were over, she carried supplies to the ward where she resided and in the evenings worked on projects.

"One project was significantly different from the others. In this project she learned a new skill and needed instruction. The task was to cover a velvet belt with many leather snaps in a decorative fashion. In this task small actions repeated many times over led to a successfully completed whole. She could pursue small efforts that culminated in something larger. She was totally preoccupied with the task and derived a wholesome pleasure in doing it."[6]

This occupational therapy program seen in its entirety revealed two variants of high tension levels in Mrs. A.'s behavior. Early in her hospitalization, her sessions were marked by excitement, that is, by disorganized activity. Later, especially when the staff discovered the kind of task and social arrangements that gave productive form to her needs, Mrs. A. was able to channel her energies and become more focused and alive.

We can fill up any period of time in our lives, an afternoon or a week, with a range of separate behaviors. To the degree that we can organize our actions into purposeful wholes, we build both complexity and unity into that period of time. Insofar as we cannot master these separate pieces of our lives, we find that at best we do many isolated things that have their own intensity, but we cannot know thorough aliveness. It takes coherently organized activity for that.

Thorough aliveness is characterized by a balance of person's urge toward self-assertion and his or her simultaneous urge to become part of a larger entity by merging into it.

To be thoroughly alive, a person must express in a balanced form both of two major trends of organic life. One of these trends is the urge toward *self-assertion;* the other, *mergence striving,* is the effort to merge into a group of persons beyond the self or to merge into nature. When a person is all alive, then, he has solved for that moment the key dialectic of declaring his uniqueness with reference to others but also of losing himself in the specialness of the group created by all the participants. He is simultaneously and equally defining himself through the assertion of his idiosyncratic nature, and losing himself through his union with others in his field of action.[7]

The idea of "assertion" means the action of declaration, of putting forth, so that *self-assertion* as a trend is manifested by actions of declaring oneself. Individuals are self-assertive from infancy throughout their life spans. Their autonomous statements of self begin with temperament at birth. Some babies communicate that they are soothed by touch, others by murmuring sounds, still others only by nursing. The wise parent learns the self-defining characteristics of his child in order to satisfy the child's needs, thus nurturing wholesome development of the self-assertive trend. As each stage in development unfolds, the child, as well as the parent, regulates her growth through self-declaring, autonomous efforts. All of life is endowed with the ever-increasing capacity to articulate self and to define and declare its particularity. Identity formation is a life-long process, and we become increasingly skilled at it the longer we live.

Similarly, if we understand the notion of "merging" to mean that something loses its character or identity in something else, then *mergence striving* is expressed by actions in which a person loses her own character or identity by combining with other persons in collective effort. As persons are self-assertive from infancy onwards, so too they continuously seek to unite themselves with others in mutually satisfying relations that build upon but also surpass their separateness. The infant nursing with her mother, the three-year old children engrossed in common play, the juvenile's attention to her chums, adolescents exploring intimacy exemplify the trend toward merging which accompanies all actions and encounters and which is as dominant a part of the self as the urge toward autonomy.

The balanced organization of self-assertion and mergence striving calls for declaration of self as an affirmative act and loss of self by unity with a collective endeavor. A violin concerto demands of the soloist and the orchestra just such interplay of the two trends. The soloist is the leading individual among a set of individuals. She is expected to assert her special talents in the parts of the concerto written for her. Sometimes she plays alone, sometimes with one or several other instruments, sometimes with the whole orchestra, varying, therefore, the actions that emphasize her separateness and uniqueness within the whole performance. Yet, if the soloist is overbearing, if she parades her talents without regard to her place in the orchestra as a group, she fails in her mergence striving and she does not provide us with a moving performance. What is important is the blending of the instruments in which the collective takes up the individuality and unique contributions of the soloist as well as each member of the orchestra. We discover not only the special sounds of the soloist's violin, but the different offerings of the others, the oboe, the kettle drums, violas and cellos, and we find all these in a higher accomplishment, an attainment in which it becomes unclear and unimportant to identify exactly who did what.

People in our society seem to believe that self-assertion is the only aspect that defines individuality. That is to say, individuality is equated with declaring the uniqueness of self. We are thought to be expressing our private character only when we set ourselves off from others. I am suggesting here, however, that individuality is a function of a person's methods of merging with others just as it is a function of his self-assertions. It requires that we open ourselves to embeddedness in a social unit while we close the circle of our separateness. Both facets are necessary to defining our individuality.

In all behavior there is self-assertion and mergence striving. But it is the balance of these urges that distinguishes whether a person is able to become thoroughly alive. With balance the person feels united and all alive, and with imbalance, he feels either deadness, agitation or oscillation between the two. The trends are balanced when each is utilized in action and when each supports the other, In other words, a person is defining and declaring his autonomy in such a manner that he facilitates his incorporation into social solidarity; he is seeking to merge with the collective unit by bringing special contributions to it.

The trends are imbalanced when each is antagonistic to the other so that if one trend is manifested the other trend cannot appear at the same time. In the state of imbalance, the person may be declaring her uniqueness over against her drive to merge with others, or the person may be seeking to secure necessary satisfactions by renouncing her particular, self-assertive qualities in favor of the effort to become submerged. When we call someone selfish, we believe that he cares more for safeguarding his individuality than building his cooperation with others. Usually so-called selfish people are uncertain about their separateness and are unclear about their impact on the world, so they exaggerate their autonomous efforts in ways that defeat their attempts to get along with others. On the other side, some people seem too readily to identify their fate with a group, too eager to become obscured as individuals through submission to a group. They try to cooperate with others without asserting their special nature, often because they covertly wish to dominate or control others rather than negotiate as equals. Both the self-aggrandizing and self-abasing represent forms of imbalance between the trends toward self-assertion and mergence striving.

In the next example, a caseworker created the social relations that enabled his client to balance the trends of self-assertion and mergence striving. Other workers had previously failed to foster the coordination of these trends for the client, with extremely negative results.

Example 3. Mr. Elkins is a caseworker in a public assistance agency. He has not received professional training, so that his gifted work with clients is his own creation throughout. I had the opportunity to talk with him about some of the people he has served when I was working on research concerning some personality characteristics of persons who are clients of public assistance agencies. The following story comes from one of our discussions.

Mr. Elkins was the fourth, or possibly the fifth or sixth, caseworker assigned to work with Mr. Jaspers. Mr. Jaspers, now forty-five years old, was a dark-skinned black bachelor whose life had been very difficult from its beginning and whose present-day habits were frightening. He had had several head injuries when young and had been hit by a car. He had been in jail for four years, convicted of assault and battery with intent to kill. For several months prior to that he had been in a state mental hospital, diagnosed as a paranoid personality problem and considered dangerous. He lived alone. He frequently threatened to kill people and had stopped Mr. Elkins' predecessor, a young woman, on the street, had demanded favors and had threatened her.

Mr. Elkins, after studying the records concerning Mr. Jaspers, discovered that every time someone tried to boss him or dictate to him, he burst into a rage and threatened attack. Each new caseworker, for example, would talk with Mr. Jaspers about his unemployment or his inability to hold a job and would begin to direct Mr. Jaspers along some course of action. The response was consistently negative. Mr. Elkins decided, accordingly, that it was unwise to dictate to Mr. Jaspers. "I plan to tell him I don't make the rules — I only carry them out." Mr. Elkins recalled the implementation of his plan:

"I was prepared to go along with him. If he wanted to talk about employment, I let him talk about it, but I was ready to interject what I wanted to know. I told him we were not asking him to seek employment since times were hard. For years we had insisted on employment and this insistence had set him off. He said he did not have enough money to live on. I agreed and explained the policies and limitations on us. I told him that I was not there to run his life; that he was to do this as he saw it.

"The next visit he asked me to take him to a nearby town where he could apply for some work that was not continuing but that became available periodically. I readily agreed to drive him, and the simple, speedy agreement astonished him. He asked, 'Why are you doing this for me?' I replied that I had told him the first time I had met him that I was there to help him help himself. He answered, in turn, 'Nobody else ever did this for me.'

"During that trip I learned more about him than I have learned about any single client during one visit. In a trusting, confidential, friendly manner he unburdened himself to me. I learned that his father died when he was young; his mother, wanting to keep the family together, married a man who did not like him and who beat him regularly. His stepfather despised him for his dark skin color, which was darkest in all the family, and for his mental limits. His brothers and sisters were treated better than he, and his relations to them deteriorated. And on and on he went. He was warm, personal and intimate and not one bit aggressive. I discovered that he was sorely afraid of authority...."

Mr. Elkins fostered in his client balance of the two trends of self-assertion and mergence striving. The other caseworkers had made these trends take on an antagonistic character within Mr. Jaspers by their insistence that he find employment or lose public-assistance funding. Under these demands, if Mr. Jaspers sought work, he could meet his mergence striving through submission to the requirements but he would have to deny his own drive toward that end, that is, his own self-assertive motivation to be employed. Even though he sincerely desired to work, as shown by his initiative in respect to employment when Mr. Elkins removed the public-assistance pressure, he could not demonstrate this earlier because the caseworkers wanted him to work on their terms, not his.

Thorough aliveness is characterized by the creation of mutual bonds between the person and others.

The construction of new unities with others, new mutual understandings, or positive joint labors, is always a component part of thorough aliveness. These mutual bonds may be unencumbered by differences among the participants or they may be forged from the materials of grave disagreement and painful struggles. Some of my closest moments with others have come when we have hurt each other deeply and yet have been able to share the hurt we felt and transcended our differences. Thorough aliveness is characterized by a resultant harmony but the unity of experience may evolve from tough reciprocal actions as well as congenial ones.

The mutual bonding process among people is central to thorough aliveness and also to equalitarian relationships. In my Introduction I have differentiated uses of authority by their concern for reciprocity and inclusiveness in equalitarianism versus the gaining of an advantage in a competitive forum in authoritarianism. Equalitarianism involves assumptions of mutual inclusiveness of benefits, coordination of differences and maximizing goal achievements. Authoritarianism rests on assumptions that authority is used to collect and defend one's satisfactions in the world of inequality. Authority tied to exclusive gains is authoritarian, and it is clearly not the type of authority that most nurtures the togetherness of people. Based on expectations of win-lose relations, authoritarianism inhibits the unfolding of mutuality. The aim toward mutual bonding is central to equalitarianism and people are more likely to become thoroughly alive in equalitarian relationships than in authoritarian ones.

In the next example we see the development of a deep tie under unlikely circumstances. An adolescent woman, confined in an institution partly because she had been rebellious in reference to authorities, is subjected to forceful, though equalitarian, use of authority. From the encounter she had an experience of thorough aliveness.

Example 4. In an article called "Institutional Social Education of Severely Maladjusted Girls," Asger Hansen writes:

"One morning in 1960, an intelligent seventeen-year-old girl reacted with a violent emotional and aggressive outburst to a minor disappointment. I was called at about 10:30 a.m., at which time she was breaking windows and furniture in her room. When she saw me, she demanded in a very excited way to be placed in the isolation room.

"At 4:30 p.m. that afternoon she wanted to have a conversation with me. During about 1½ hours we discussed very thoroughly her basic situation. She spoke quietly without affective overtones. There was a long history of well-established hostile relationships with authorities, primarily with her father but also with all representatives of social agencies, including teachers, police, child and welfare workers, etc. She showed a good understanding of the fact that, when frustrated, she reacted with regression to an infantile pattern of defiance. We talked about the normal stubbornness of small children and compared her own behavioral pattern with this tendency.

"Toward the end of the conversation, which occurred in an atmosphere of very good contact, she asked if she could leave the isolation room. I answered in the negative, about as follows: 'You knew that I did not like to use the isolation room, but you forced me to it. I do not use this room for petty disciplinary nonsense. If I really have to use it, it will be for at least twenty-four hours. I consider you a grown-up human being, and grown-up people have the right to be reacted to in a grown-up way. This implies that you cannot play truant with respect to the consequences of your own behavior. Had you been the little child of four we talked about just now, I should have taken pity and removed you at once, but you are an adult, and therefore you have to be isolated until 10:30 tomorrow morning.'

"Her reaction to this explanation was a very quiet 'Thank you,' after which she equally quietly went back to the isolation room. Later on she told me that on this occasion, for the first time, she felt respected as an adult human being and not treated as an irresponsible child."[9]

What is significant about this encounter was Hansen's ability to harmonize the girl's regressive behavior and the realistic demands of the institution in a linkage that respected the integrity of the girl as well as the institution. He accepted the girl's urgent call for isolation, allowing her to become quiet alone, away from excessive stimulation, apart from destructiveness. Thus, he had responsively approved the wisdom of her decision. Because he had agreed to her request, he was empowered by her to tie her requirement to the needs of the institution, which he defined as the use of the isolation room only in extreme circumstances. He could very well have interpreted her call for isolation either as an emergency, short-run, impetuous solution of a child asking for parental control, or as an emergency solution in which a needy person used available resources to secure mastery over her destructive and self-destructive behavior. When Hansen chose the second interpretation and communicated his understanding to the girl, he was permitting her to direct the situation within the limitations and context of the institution.

In this encounter Hansen was not simply imposing his power upon her arbitrarily as other authorities had done in the past, but rather placed the facilities of the organization at her service as long as she made positive use of them. The girl was given command of her daily life, which she needed desperately because she mistrusted the power of authority to take advantage of her. Hansen enabled the girl to unite her self-assertive and mergence tendencies and to unite with him and the institution at the same time. In addition, he was able to use his influence well with someone who was hypersensitive to people in power.

In the context of these characteristics of thorough aliveness and the examples that portray them, the idea that all human interactions result in roughly equal amounts of satisfaction for every participant may be more plausible. Most people I know are skeptical about the idea. It does not seem to agree with either their experience or their common sense. When presented with the notion, people adamantly insist on definitive proof. Furthermore, they register more than simple disbelief in the proposition; they seem to resist or actively dislike the idea. They do not seem to want it to be true that equalization of satisfactions is the inevitable outcome of interactions. To accept the idea that no one is only victim or only oppressor undermines people's basic assumptions about human nature and social existence. Were they to accept the idea of equalization, they might be forced to reorder their entire perspective.

There are times, also, when I think people fear to accept the idea because they want to avoid disappointment. Better to assume the worst, that people are inconsiderate or downright self-centered, they seem to say, so that one is prepared when exploitation actually does occur. Equality of satisfactions appears to be associated in their minds with some naive sense of the goodness of people, and they act as if assuming that people are fundamentally programmed toward equalizing makes one unwisely gullible.

Yet these examples I have presented reveal this equality *when we look to find it.* Not only Deborah, Mrs. A., Mr. Jaspers and the adolescent girl underwent the transformation from inadequate existence to greater aliveness. The same change occurred for the other relevant persons in the events: Carla, the occupational therapists, Mr. Elkins and Mr. Hansen. We did not notice this because we tend to assume that there are primary beneficiaries in encounters, and we thus do not appraise the satisfactions experienced by those whom we consider secondary gainers. We impose our expectations of inequality upon our very observation and evaluation of events.

In two of the examples, I personally observed the satisfactions experienced by the authorities — by the occupational therapists, e.g., when Mrs. A. was guided into the task that animated her existence and Mr. Elkins' pleasures in his contacts with Mr. Jaspers. I talked with these people about their reactions to the events they described, and in both instances, the aliveness of the authorities paralleled that of the persons of their concern. When Mrs. A. and Mr. Jaspers felt full aliveness, so did the occupational therapists and Mr. Elkins. When they were dissatisfied, so were the helpers. The amount of satisfaction for the participants expanded and contracted together.

There is a problem with these examples to which I must respond. The outcomes in each of them were positive and easily seen as mutual. There was no obvious attempt at exploitation in them. The critical cases in reference to the equalization thesis are those in which aggrandizement seems to be taking place, in which it appears that one participant is victimizing the others. Particularly relevant in explaining why equalizing happens even when inequality is intended are the two characteristics of the balancing of self-assertion and mergence strivings and the bonding of person with others.

This two-directional process, in which each person regulates his self-assertive and mergence strivings within himself while simultaneously regulating his relations with other persons, contains the mechanisms which bring about equal satisfactions for participants in transactions. Each actor in an event must deal with his own internal trends of self-assertion and mergence striving. Moreover, in relating to another person, he must also contend with these same urges as manifested by the other. Thus, each person faces his own self-assertion plus the self-assertion of others, and each manages his own efforts to merge into a larger unit while dealing with the parallel strivings of the remaining persons in the interaction. The interdependence of people in an encounter around these trends either causes them to flourish together or commonly diminish the levels of satisfaction that they can achieve.

Social and psychological literature is replete with theories that pose the fundamental problems between the individual and others, between instincts and civilization, between the citizen and the state. In effect, these dichotomies ignore the importance of the divisions within each individual and the contradictions within the collectivity. These are truncated theories that necessarily distort our perceptions of reality. Self-other conflicts are also always self-self conflicts. It is not sufficiently recognized that differences between the individual and society are at the same time problems within society and problems within the individuals who wish to merge with the society.

Although Freud is one of the leading thinkers who is generally understood to endorse the view that instincts and civilization are inherently antagonistic, one of his discussions on this topic is surprisingly close to the view I am arguing here. He writes:

> "The development of the individual seems to us to be a product of the interaction between the two urges, the urge towards happiness, which we usually call 'egoistic,' and the urge towards union with others in the community, which we call 'altruistic.'"

Here, his "egoistic" equals what I have called self-assertion and his "altruistic" what I have named mergence striving. Further on, Freud continues:

> "So, also, the two urges, the one towards personal happiness and the other towards union with other human beings, must struggle with each other in every individual; and so, also, the two processes of individual and of cultural development must stand in hostile opposition to each other and mutually dispute the ground."[9]

The helpful part of Freud's conception here is his observation that the two urges in the individual are independent of each other and yet must be accommodated to each other, and his similar insight that the processes of the individual as a system and of culture as a system at another level of organization are independent yet in constant interplay. He portrays the background for the two-directional regulatory activity that appears in every action by laying out the independent status of egoism and altruism (self-assertion and mergence striving) and the separate status of individual and culture. As independent factors, these may be reciprocally adapted so that balance is achieved or they may become antagonistic to each other. We create this balance or imbalance in our actions.

What is less helpful, indeed mischievous in its ramifications, is Freud's view that these independent trends are always exclusive and competitive. He implies that egoism cannot be integrated in a balanced way with altruism and that the individual and culture can never be fully reconciled or mutually supportive. He goes on to say that the independent urges and processes "must struggle," "stand in hostile opposition," and "mutually dispute."

But it is one thing to say that forces are independent of each other and another thing to say that they are irreconcilable. Because they are independent, self-assertion and mergence striving (or individual and culture) are not automatically connected in a balanced form. They are always potentially anatagonistic. By the same token, however, they are always potentially mutually supportive or balanced. This everpresent possibility of balance between the independent forces is missed by Freud and others who tell us that instincts and civilization necessarily oppose each other.

Indeed, living as an organic phenomenon consists of the dialectic process in which the two urges within the individual and the individual-cultural forces assert their independence and are brought into coordination. We pulsate from the alternation in which now they are integrated, now distinct and independent. Just when we think we have tied our self-assertions productively with our urge to unite with others, we try to complicate or extend what we declare of ourselves or we try to merge with a larger group. The independence of these factors then brings us to reshape their balance.

When we forego the oversimplification and pay attention to both self-assertion and mergence striving, and to these two trends in all collaborators in an interaction, we better understand the process of equalization of satisfaction even when one person is trying to exploit another. When one person tries to aggrandize herself with respect to another, she learns that she does not simply gain while the other loses. Her self-assertion and the other's submission in the service of collaboration (that is, the other's mergence striving) are complementary but they comprise only half of what takes place.

Since a person always experiences the two needs of asserting the self and merging with others simultaneously, the aggrandizing individual discovers that she must actively suppress her own mergence striving because union with others and aggrandizing are incompatible. Although it is possible, indeed desirable, to define oneself and yet lose oneself in a larger common cause, that is, to express self-assertion and mergence striving in a balanced way, it is not possible to declare oneself *at the expense of the other* and yet merge with him. Self-aggrandizement is negation of the individuality of the other person, especially of his self-assertive drive, and by negating the other, the aggrandizer forfeits a larger unit that combines the self-declarations of all participants.

Many alcoholics are entangled in this problematic aggrandizing style of activity. They are egocentric, willful, possessed with an exaggerated sense of their own importance, exceedingly self-reliant and often bullying of others. When they pull back from this exploitative stance, they go to the other extreme of helplessness, disavowal of responsibility, passivity and dependence. When the alcoholic is egocentric, he cares little for union with others; when he is passive, he is completely submerged vis-a-vis others and is overly determined by them. His incapacity to balance the two trends is basic to his problem. The same theme prevails in persons entwined in sadistic-masochistic interactions.

Thus, for one person to exploit another, he must negotiate the two trends within himself in order to promote self-assertion and deny the expression of his trend toward union with others; concurrently, he must negotiate with the other person in his effort to foster the other's mergence striving and encourage the suppression of the other's self-assertion. To aggrandize is to advance one's own will and disown one's own desires for surrender while promoting the other's self-sacrificing cooperation. That is why the exploiter must maintain an image of toughness and self-control. He must communicate his invulnerability toward his own desire for union with others as well as his determination to punish the self-declarative intentions of others.

The relation of the alcoholic man and his wife, as commonly seen by clinicians, reflects the complementary and comparable aspects of internal conflict. An alcoholic is often overly self-assertive and frequently abusive toward his wife. (In our society men are encouraged more in their self-assertiveness, women more in their mergence striving. As this changes, so too there is increase in alcoholism and spouse abuse in women.) The alcoholic's wife, however fearfully, is overly submissive and loyal. Outsiders wonder why she tolerates the abuse she receives, but over time come to realize that she not only tolerates it, she is covertly a party to it. When the alcoholic then becomes abashed and contrite, he sooner or later finds himself manipulated into drinking by his wife and follows her hidden directions as if he had no will of his own. Perverse though it be, it is her turn to dominate. Husband and wife need each other because they pick up for each other the half of themselves which is suppressed. Back and forth they go, often over many years, first with his self-assertion wedded to her mergence striving, then with the reverse, in a consistent but unstable and painful pattern. Although clearly with unsatisfactory and discordant results, they equalize their satisfactions while complementing each other.

But relations of aggrandizement-sacrifice, dominance-submission, sadism-masochism, one up-one down, exploiter-exploited, oppressor-oppressed lead to relatively low levels of satisfaction because they introduce internal contradictions in the psychological functioning of those who participate in the relations. Because the contradictions within the participants are complementary and comparable, equalization of these low levels of satisfaction follows. Where one person is self-assertive and unconcerned with union, the other is centered upon merging and divorced from his own self-assertive trend. The overemphasis upon self-assertion in the first person is matched by the overemphasis upon mergence striving in the other. The denial of the urge to unite is paralleled by the denial of the urge toward self-declaration. Since both self-assertion and mergence striving are fundamental parts of the self, both must be affirmed in a relationship, and when both are, full aliveness is maximized.

In studying the qualities of thorough aliveness, I have avoided the customary examples. I have not relied upon instances of romantic love, high artistic inspiration, breathtaking athletic feats, religious wonders or acquisition of great political or social power. Life belongs to the everyday, the mundane, the details. So many of us have become accustomed to the injustice and impoverishment of our daily social relations that we look to special events and occasions for vitality. Yet every aspect of living is available to us if we understand the principles that produce thorough aliveness. The great moments occur infrequently, the little ones all day long, every day. If we depend upon the great and momentous times, we assign ourselves too little pleasure. We would do well to attend in new ways to the large and small possibilities as they present themselves in our lives. There is more space for the creation of vital aliveness than we have begun to imagine.

Notes

1. This is a modified presentation of an article of the same name published in *et cetera*, 1980, Volume 37.

2. James C. Fernald. *Funk and Wagnalls Standard Handbook of Synonyms, Antonyms and Prepositions*. New York: Funk and Wagnalls, 1947.

3. Abraham H. Maslow. *Toward a Psychology of Being*. New York: Van Nostrand, 1962.

4. Hannah Green. *I Never Promised You a Rose Garden*. New York: Holt, Rinehart and Winston, 1964.

5. Josef Breuer and Sigmund Freud. *Studies on Hysteria*. In: *The Standard Edition of the Complete Psychological Works of Sigmund Freud, Volume II*. James Strachey, General Editor. London: Hogarth Press, 1955.

6. Cynthia Board, Jane King and Anna Marie Tierney with Philip Lichtenberg, "Time Perspective and Intimacy: Their Effect on Patient Behavior in Occupational Therapy." *A.M.A. Archives of General Psychiatry*, 1959, Volume 1.

7. Cf. Andras Angyal, *Neurosis and Treatment: A Holistic Theory*, New York: Wiley, 1965, for an analysis very much like the one being developed here. He specifies the operation of two trends as defining the dynamic principles of growth: the trend toward autonomy, life as a process of self-expansion, and the trend toward homonomy, life as a process of placing oneself in a larger unit of which one becomes a part.

8. Asger Hansen. "Institutional Social Education of Severely Maladjusted Girls." In: *International Trends in Mental Health*. Henry P. David, Editor. New York: McGraw–Hill, 1966.

9. Sigmund Freud. *Civilization and Its Discontents*. In: *The Standard Edition of the Complete Psychological Works of Sigmund Freud, Volume 21*. James Strachey, General Editor. London: Hogarth Press, 1955.

CHAPTER 4

THIRD PARTY INFLUENCE

"It has been facetiously suggested that... every community and industry should be required to place its water intake downstream from its outfall."[1]

"I want to call attention to one of Czechoslovakia's regulations that borders on genius: 'A plant's water intake is to be downstream of its discharge.'"[2]

Many years ago I lived in a working-class neighborhood in a town in the southern suburbs of Chicago, near the Indiana border. At that time the town had only recently changed from a small, rural community where farm machinery was sold and serviced into a growing suburban center composed mainly of small, development ranch houses with common interior layouts and only slightly varying exterior facades. An expressway cut through the northern section of town, not far from the house I had hastily acquired during a sudden move, and this expressway made Chicago an easily accessible city. Most of the newcomers to the town, my neighbors, had moved out from Chicago in order to put distance between themselves and the black population of the city, a fact I discovered only after I had moved in from an apartment in New York City.

In addition to their extreme prejudice and a strong, fundamentalist religiosity, their lives were marked by a fascinating and puzzling intimacy. A significant proportion of the women in the neighborhood visited each other regularly for morning coffee and during the course of their conversation would often discuss in great detail their sexual experiences with their husbands. They shared openly, with much descriptiveness and feeling, what might be thought to be the most personal of all their experiences. These were not liberated women; they were conventional, repressed, hard-working, anti-psychological, generally conservative people, so that their open and explicit sexual descriptions were all the more unexpected.

In schematic form, the typical episode was this: One woman became connected with another woman in respect to her previous sexual experience with a man, her husband. When we formulate this triangular episode in psychological terms, we discover a strange ambiguity. The woman telling her story may have been trying to master an experience that was both attractive and frightening to her, relating it in a context that was distant from, and more safe than, the sexual encounter itself. If this were the situation, then the interest of the woman telling her tale was focused upon her husband and her sexual relations with him, and we would outline the event in the following way:

A wife examines her wife-husband relation with the assistance of another woman.

The purpose of such a conversation might be to receive ideas, evaluations and judgments which would confirm her own, which would add to her understanding or which would prepare her for future sexual relations with her husband. In such an instance, her husband would be a central part of the subject matter of the conversation and the direct object of the talk as well, despite his physical absence at the moment. The other woman, who listened to the story and gave her counsel, would be *a third party* to the wife-husband connection.

Another perspective on these intimate conversations may be discerned, however, one equally as plausible as the previous description. Possibly the woman was directing her sexual interest and involvement *toward her morning listener* in a way that disguised the purpose but allowed its appearance. It could have been that the woman used stories about her husband as a means for arousing sexual feelings in the other as someone might use pornography, love poems or perfume. If this second option were true, then the interest of the speaker was centered upon the other woman and the encounter would be outlined differently:

A woman relates to another woman around sexuality by the assistance of tales recounting her relations with her husband.

The purpose of this conversation, then, would have been to experience homosexual feelings without awareness of this intent. The fact that the subject matter was heterosexual would have acted to obscure the actual homosexual involvement. In this case the husband, although part of the subject matter of the event, would not have been the direct object of it and the listener would not have been a third party. The woman would be less concerned with sex-and-her-husband, more attracted to sex-and-her-coffee-partner.

It was not clear to me whether the coffee mate was a third party to the narrator's sexual interests or the object of them. What did the story teller want from her friend? There was definite unclarity in the situation. It boiled down to a question of who were the real participants in the interaction and what indeed was the function of the other figure, the third party.

As I puzzled about this third party influence, I happened upon a discussion of mother-child relations that seemed to me to illuminate that matter. In *The Freudian Wish*,[3] published in 1915, Edwin B. Holt shaped a psychological base for ethics in what I consider to be a magnificent rendering of a central theme in psychoanalysis. In Chapter III of his book, "The Wish in Ethics," Holt articulates connections between suppression, dissociation and discrimination, and his argument helps to define what is meant by third party influence upon a person's relation to an object.

For Holt, Freud's concept of wish refers to "any purpose or project *for a course of action.*" Any suppression of wishes, according to Freud, leads to dissociation within the person suppressing himself. There can be no suppression of a project for a course of action that would be free from the cost of dissociation; all self-renunciation breaks apart the integration of the person. Because dissociation invokes contradictions within the person, it leads to faulty conduct:

"The simultaneous excitation of dissociated (i.e., antagonistic) paths by one stimulus that is harmful."

In terms I have been using, dissociation fosters excitement rather than incitement, activation of many forces that are not coherently organized.

"And now we can see how and why suppressions occur in this world of ours. It is through lack of knowledge. Our first contact with objects presents us with anomalies, contradictions, perplexities. Until further experience teaches us to discriminate further particulars within these objects, we shall be in some degree the victims of suppression, and our conduct will be to some extent equivocal, immoral."

In contrast to suppression of wishes and the consequent dissociation, Holt describes the moral condition which he believes is the expression of all wishes in the context of discrimination. Discrimination leads to knowledge of particulars, including awareness of differences and agreements among persons, obstacles and facilitations to getting what one wants, and through such knowledge to reconciliation, resolution or intergration.

"Right is that conduct attained through discrimination of the facts, which fulfills all of a man's wishes at once, suppressing none.... The doctrine of the wish shows us... that we shall play the game of life rightfully if, instead of so painfully scrutinizing and trying to suppress our wishes, we turn about and lucidly discriminate the facts."

This ethics, which eschews all suppression and its accompanying dissociation in favor of *integrated* inclusiveness, is accompanied by an analysis of third party control of discrimination. In the example Holt uses, it is clear that the mother is what I call a third party.

"An innate tendency or purpose of an infant is to put out its hand to touch fire. If the mother is by, she holds back the hand (*her* purpose) before it reaches the flame. There is a hint for the child, here, of right and wrong. If the mother guards the child unremittingly, and every time restrains the hand before the uncomfortable warmth begins to stimulate the child's own tendency to withdraw, the child will never be burned and may eventually... acquire the habit of stopping short before reaching the flame. But this cautious conduct will not be guided by (be a function of) the heat of the flame, for the child has had no experience of this. The child's general conduct toward the fire will then be partly a function of the immediate properties of fire (its color, position, shape, etc.): but partly also of a something else (really its mother), which may or may not figure explicitly in the child's field of consciousness. The mother has set a barrier between the child and a portion of reality; and forever after the child will be in some measure impeded in its dealings with fire....

"Or again, if an equally unremitting mother lets the child put its hand toward the flame and takes care only that the hand by too great momentum or an accidental lurch does not actually come into the flame, the child will not be burned and its own mechanism of withdrawal will be exercised not through the mother's interference but through the direct action of the flame's heat. The child's conduct toward fire becomes integrated, and is solely a function of the actual properties of fire. Ten years later you shall hear the first mother shouting, 'Bobbie, don't you dare put your hand so near the lamp, and if you touch those matches again your father will whip you.' And the second mother will be saying, 'Bobbie, go get the matches now and light the lamp, and set it down on the center-table.'"

The two mothers in Holt's discussion act very differently and their behavior suggests properties that demarcate third parties to any relationship. The one mother brings about a suppression of the wish to explore the flame and she causes dissociation in the child from confusion about who is the primary object, the fire or the mother. The child is prevented from developing an integrated action because of the (authoritarian) intrusion of the mother. The second mother supervises the child, serves as a means toward greater knowledge of the properties of the fire, but she allows the child to connect with the fire in its own terms. She facilitates expression of the child's wish and its integrated development, using what I call equalitarian authority.

A third party to an interaction between a person and her object is defined by two characteristics. First, the individual who is a third party exerts influence of some kind upon the person and her relation to an object. The first mother directly controls her child's behavior in regard to the fire. In the terms I have been using in these essays, a third party exercises authority. Second, however, a third party differs from other participants in relationships in the asymmetrical flow of influence. A third party exerts some degree of control over the person-object relationship but is not reciprocally influenced or controlled by that relationship. This means she is a determiner of the relation to others but is not determined by these others. Consequently, the third party is both in the relationship and separate from it, associated but also removed from it, a part of it but also apart from it.

The first mother is clearly a third party in that she affects the child's relation to the fire but is not determined by the child or the fire. If the child, in his confusion, gives up interest in the fire and attends to his mother alone, she in no longer a third party — there is no separate person-object relation upon which she can intrude. But as long as the child must accommodate both to the fire and to his mother without concurrently having authority and accountability in respect to his mother, he is embedded in a third party situation.

The second mother in Holt's discussion may be a third party, if she "takes care" intrusively, that is, she may be an authority relatively immune to the influence attempts of the child, or she may be merely another figure in the child-fire-mother relationship, by creating a situation of mutual accountability. This mother lets the child tell her when he needs her and is generally responsive to his initiatives. The ideal, as I see it, and at which Holt hints, would be no third-party activity, only mutual regulation among all participants in relationship to each other.

A third party may invade either more or less into the interaction between a person and the object of his interest. A third party can be more or less controlling of that relationship or intrusive upon it. The degree of intrusiveness that the third party represents is paralleled by how much spontaneity and mutuality is permitted to exist in the interaction. We are alerted by Holt's anecdote also to the idea that third party influence seems to be especially important in new experiences or unfamiliar circumstances. The effects of third party influence are also particularly powerful, as I came to realize from my neighbors in Chicago, according to principles and institutions that emphasize the need for authoritarian control.

One method of estimating the extent of third party influence entails measuring (1) the proportion of the transaction between a person and her object directly determined by forces emanating from the third party, and (2) the proportion that is a function solely of factors contributed by the person and the object in their interplay.[4] The range of this intrusiveness of the third party can reach from full control of events in the person-other relation, as exemplified by the dominating mother in Holt's example, to secondary, minor influence, as shown by the second, the assisting mother. In the first instance, the child's relation to the fire is substantially the child's reflection of the mother's relation to the fire. The child acts not from his own experience, his own perception, his own reflexes, but from the will and understanding of his mother. The rewards and punishments he obtains derive from what his mother does, not as they should, from what he directly learns and feels regarding the fire.

Harry Braverman has described the degradation of work in capitalist societies in the twentieth century according to the excessive third party intrusiveness engendered by scientific management. He argues that step by step, first in industrial enterprises and more recently in commercial and service organizations, work has been simplified and control of the interaction between the worker and materials or other persons has been taken over by management. The decline of craft and workmanship is a direct function of a steady erosion of independent transactions on the part of the worker. He refers to:

> "The pivot upon which all modern management turns: the control over work through the control over the *decisions that are made in the course of work.*"
>
> "The systematic pre-planning and pre-calculation of all elements of the labor process, which now no longer exists as a process in the imagination of the worker but only as a process in the imagination of a special management staff."[5]

If all of a person's work is designed for her beforehand, then her reactions to the raw materials or to the people who interact with her in the course of the work are no longer her own. Her behavior is no longer that of one who is an active cause of her own directions, but rather it is that of an instrument. Third party control is external authority that narrowly constrains a worker's behavior and is not reciprocally influenced by the worker.

Not all work is completely prescribed. Often there are merely guidelines or general rules available to the worker. It is suggested to him that the most efficient, effective or productive line of action consists of certain recommended behaviors. When this degree of leeway is permitted, there is less intrusion by the third party upon the details of the interaction. The worker has more space of free movement, more opportunity to consider, decide and choose actions according to the current feedback and responses he receives from the object. He is more likely to see himself as influential, as the source of some power. His rewards and punishments are somewhat less a function of the third party, more an outcome of his transaction with the other.

This minimum intrusion by a third party is exemplified by the second mother in Holt's discussion. She helps her child to have the most intense direct transaction with the object of his attention. In this, the most sound function for a third party, whatever external influence is instituted enables the individual affected to relate to the object so that the greatest knowledge unfolds, and discrimination of facts regulates person and object.

The degree of third party control has several possibilities in the picture: (1) the third party *rewards* and *punishes* particular behaviors of an individual with respect to an object; (2) the third party *suggests* or *counsels* particular behavior; (3) the third party *facilitates* spontaneous interaction between the person and object. Beyond minimum intrusion is (4) the region of participation in a mutually authoritative relationship. Individuals feel the weight of these different intrusions according to the control represented by them.

I have described third party involvements among my neighbors, between mother and child, and in management control over the labor process, and now I turn to an area in which I was working when the ideas about third party influence first came into my view. Such influence from outside, and the confusion it may stimulate, is a significant factor when people in need of help approach an institution which offers services they require, but which is new or unfamiliar to them. I was in a child psychiatry clinic studying the paths people traversed on their way to our service and looked at how potential applicants to our clinic sought advice, assistance and information in their community around a given problem as they moved along a social path towards us. For instance, a mother was faced with a behavior problem of her daughter's that she was incapable of handling fully within the family circle. She spoke with her daughter's teacher, the church leader where the family worshipped, the family physician, and the girl's friends about the problem before she eventually asked for help at our child guidance service. Many of these relationships dealing with the search for a solution to the daughter's difficulties manifested third party control.

In analyzing a number of such paths, I found a systematic incompleteness and confounding of the relation between the client and the resource helper.[6] Because many clients lacked trust, hope, and a sense of shared responsibility, they were fearful that they would be hurt by the people from whom they sought help. Many clients of social agencies still believe that they must protect themselves even from those who are presumably interested only in being of service to them, and they often try to do this by calling upon third parties. Dependence upon outside persons enables them to equalize the power in the encounters they are experiencing.

When the mother of the girl with problems spoke to her daughter's teacher, for example, she felt vulnerable to the influence of the teacher — or so it seemed. She tried to neutralize what she apparently saw as an imbalance of power favoring the teacher by attributing control over her own behavior to a third party. The teacher recommended that the daughter should see a psychiatrist, which the mother interpreted as an assertion that her daughter was crazy. Overwhelmed by that presumed diagnosis, yet seemingly afraid of disputing with the teacher, the mother asserted that she would like to follow the teacher's advice but she was unable to do so. Her husband, she alleged, was antagonistic to psychiatry and would never give his consent to such an action. By inventing this influence from her husband — stating that he was a third party who controlled her behavior — the mother empowered herself with respect to the teacher while seemingly presenting herself as helpless or determined by pressures coming from others.

In this study, and in later work in a public assistance agency, I was able to learn that the more troubled the applicant for services, and therefore the more in need of help he is, the more he will invoke or imagine himself as determined by third parties as a means of defending himself in what he perceives to be his subordinate position in unbalanced power relations. That is to say, the more disturbed applicants expect to be dominated and assume that desired goals are hard to reach. Among the methods they use to support themselves within the context of their hopeless and mistrusting expectations is this dependence upon third party influence.

Two questions invariably accompany the defensive use of third party control: (1) to whom is the applicant responding at any given time; and (2) what is the origin of his motivation to relate to a given object? Is it from within, this motivation, or is it from external source, so that it will disappear without continued exertion of pressure from that external source? When the mother spoke to the teacher, was she relating to the teacher with her husband as a real third party or one conveniently invented for the occasion? Is she more basically relating to her husband by means of the teacher-daughter relation? Or is she vacillating back and forth according to what fulfills her own intentions at any given moment? These are variations on the theme of how her actions might be related to her motivations, and they vary according to how she was utilizing third parties.

The reactions of a helper such as the teacher in this example are bound to be ambivalent. The helper must deal with the inconsistencies or insincerities that are associated with the mother's representations of her behavior as determined by third parties. The teacher could not know whether the mother truly believed her husband opposed taking the daughter to a psychiatrist or was merely presenting the husband's presumed objections as a device for neutralizing the suggestion of the teacher. If she tested the mother's sincerity, she would have revealed her mistrust of the mother and promoted antagonism; if she assumed the correctness of the mother's assertion, she might have been taken in by the mother's maneuver. In either case the teacher was caught in a web of contradictions. The teacher experienced the very substance of the mother's problems, lack of trust, hope, and sense of shared responsibility.

Of course, it could have been the case that the father of the girl actually opposed any idea of taking the child to a psychiatrist. I have suggested mostly in my discussion thus far that the mother was probably using the husband for her own ends, but it could as easily have been the case that he was a real force with which she had to contend. Under this conditions a very different transaction might have taken place between the mother and the teacher. Instead of the formula, mother-determined-by-husband versus teacher, we would have had the situation in which the mother would have had to act as a responsible figure reconciling conflicting pressures. The mother would have seen her situation as that of handling her daughter's problems with contributing influences, positive and negative, from her husband. She could have taken on herself responsibility for deciding what was to be done, consulting with her husband, the teacher, the minister, and others in the process. The father of the girl would have been a third party influence upon the mother, but not necessarily a dominating factor, or highly intrusive force. And the mother, acting responsibly, would not confuse others because she readily disclosed the facts, shared her problems, and welcomed counsel without undue submission to anyone offering help.

From many of my examples here, such as those involving mothers, management, teachers, and physicians, it can be deduced that authority and third party influence are heavily intertwined, although not identical. Because third party influence pertains to the coordination between a person and others or between a person and material objects, such influence can be said to manifest authority. At the same time, we must keep in mind that people can connect themselves in interactions or apply themselves to tasks without the supervision and control of external figures. Lovers exert authority in their sexual relations, but a third party is hardly necessary and lovers seldom think of their influence as authoritative. The relationship between a person and an object may contain all the authority that is needed without any third party control. Moreover, extra people in a relationship may become participants without becoming third parties so long as influence is reciprocal.

My analysis of third party influence facilitates a differentiation between equalitarian and authoritarian expressions of authority. With reference to degree of intrusion of a third party, equalitarian authority consists of either minimum intrusion or no third party control. An equalitarian use of authority by a third party enables participants to express themselves and to know each other in a genuine sense. Full identification of the separate needs and wishes permits the unique coordination of just these persons at this special time such that they realize in a mutually rewarding way their separate and common goals. Similarly, an equalitarian use of authority, focused less on control of others, more on developing knowledge, helps in the true discovery of all the facts appropriate to whatever decisions are made.

Third Party Influence

Yet equalitarian authority may consist of strong influence, not merely advisory or suggestive action. To see how this can take place, we can return to the girl with the behavior problem, the teacher and the girl's mother. If the girl's behavior reflects personal distress but does not disrupt the class, her teacher may speak with her mother in a permissive and non-coercive fashion. The teacher's aim would be to bring relief to the girl and facilitate the girl's ability to engage in school life with a greater sense of private well being. The teacher, whose class is not distorted by the girl's problem, can allow the mother to decide what next steps must be taken. If the girl upsets the class, however, if her behavior prevents the group from doing its work, she poses a different problem for the teacher. Under these conditions the teacher, as a responsible member of the group, must be forceful without being authoritarian. This is accomplished only if the teacher can avoid becoming a third party.

The teacher, in relating to the mother of the girl, must express the requisites of the group and the task. The teacher as a person, other students in the class, and the learning activity would be presented to the mother in their complexity with special regard to the girl's disturbing behavior. From the openly developed needs of these various elements of the circumstances, the teacher would communicate to the mother the necessity for action to be taken that would handle the problem. By focusing solely upon the girl's activities in the class, the teacher would tie authority to the personal and collective functions that appropriately guide them. He would act as a co-participant with the girl in the class situation, not as an external figure, and his intention in speaking with the mother would be to create other influences upon the girl which would allow her to function in class in a more socially constructive way. He would be speaking for the group and for himself and would not allow himself to be seen as outside the girl's disruptive realm. He would, accordingly, not be a third party.

Powerful authority is equalitarian if it is tied to the inherent demands of the task and the needs of the other participants, and gives open and honest expression to these. It is the authority of facts made known, not the willfulness of an individual.

Nor would the teacher ask the mother to become a third party in regard to the girl's behavior in class. He would not seek to have the mother threaten to punish or reward the girl for particular behavior in school. Such an effort would rob the teacher, the class and especially the girl of responsibility for what takes place in school. He would, instead, try to have the mother help the girl to become able to function cooperatively in school on her own. If this could not be done at home, then others such as helpers at a community mental health center might be called upon. The teacher might even insist on such an action or its equivalent, though the teacher can only properly require that the girl not disturb the class.

An authoritarian version of authority is based on intrusive third party control of the relation of persons and tasks. It involves suppression and dissociation. The person wielding authority replaces the pay-offs coming from the nature of the task and from the personal relationships among people by doling out rewards and punishements.

For example, an authoritarian teacher would call upon the mother

39

as punishment for the girl's behavior in class. He would ignore his part of the situation, demand that the mother take specific action or be reproached, act as a third party to the family's resolution of the difficulty. He would make his authority too important to the persons involved, to the detriment of knowledge about the task and information about the wishes of the participants.

The ethics of equalitarianism and authoritarianism are, in Holt's terms, ethics "from below" and "from above" respectively. We can see the point from his discussion of ethics "from above:"

> "The ethics 'from above' are a very different story. There Someone exhorts or obliges us to suppress our wishes, and if we observe Someone a bit carefully we shall all too soon often find that he generally busied *himself* with suppressing the facts. Ethics from above come indeed from above, from the man or the institution 'higher up.' And for this there is a very frail and human reason, which no one need go very far to discover. According to the ethics from below, the unassuming ethics of the dust, facts are the sole moral sanction: and facts impose the most inexorable moral penalties."[7]

One final subject matter connected with third party influence draws our attention: racism and sexism. Intrusive third party influence is the essence of racism and of sexism. When an individual acts in a racist or sexist fashion, he reveals himself to be dominated not by the facts of the other but by a third party. Rather than discriminating the individuality of those who are the object of his racist or sexist behavior, the person leans upon stereotypes formulated by some reference group to which he belongs. A person acting as a racist or sexist will not bother to learn the details about those who are the objects of his actions and thus will not be able to relate to these persons in a differentiated form.

We use the concept "racism" when we mean that blacks, Puerto-Ricans, Mexican-Americans, Native Americans, Asian-Americans and other Third World persons are improperly excluded from certain activities, positions in organizations, residential areas, or when we believe that persons so identified are inequitably rewarded and punished by the results of collective work. Similarly, we mean by "sexism" that women or gay people are excluded or treated to unequal conditions or rewards and punishments for being women or gay by virtue of irrelevant consideration of the sex differentiation or sex preference.

Analysis of racism and sexism as instances of third party intrusion upon person-other relations points up some of their basic properties. First of all, there are degrees of racism and sexism which are measured by the extent of control exerted by the third parties to which the racist or sexist owes his allegiance. When a parent punishes a child for playing with someone of a disfavored race, the parent greatly invades the child's space of free movement. The parent reveals deep racism by this constriction of the child's life. When boys are teased about their interest in girls, there is minor sexism involved, compared, for example, to the prohibition against women executives in prestigious business institutions. Racism and sexism may be surface issues in one community, basic issues in another.

A second property of racism and sexism is that they are customarily manifested in new and unfamiliar relationships. On the one hand, racism and sexism are systematically inculcated in children. Some of the most insistent expressions of racist and sexist practices are found in the training of children by adults. Parents often teach their children to dislike foreigners, blacks and others, or to assume that women must be housewives. On the other hand, a great proportion of conflicts that have evolved from efforts to combat sexism and racism concern entrance barriers — new patterns of entry to schools, jobs, restaurants and bars, and residential centers. The new and the strange are powerful components of racist and sexist tendencies.

Sexism and racism breed in authoritarian social structures. The inevitability of sexism and racism, often accompanied by fundamentalist religion, in authoritarian environments results from the fact that they are different manifestations of intrusive third party control. Societies in which work and family life are built upon principles of heavy third party domination, whether capitalist or socialist in name, seem fated to suffer from sexism and racism. When people become adapted to non-reciprocal authority patterns, they use these patterns throughout their lives. This is especially fostered when work and family life have authoritarian structures because most individuals spend the bulk of their time in either one or the other of these settings.

These observations on racism and sexism take me back to my neighbors in the suburbs of Chicago because my neighbors carried many racist and sexist tendencies. Most of them worked in autocratic institutions. Their religion was mainly of an orthodox, fundamentalist, rigid character. Their family affairs were lived through dominations and manipulations. As I remember these people, I am reminded of the depth of ambivalence they aroused in me during the whole time I lived in that community. I liked most of my neighbors most of the time; I found many reasons for affinity and mutual concern. We shared much and we got on well. It was among the better times in my life.

Yet I was perpetually angry about their explicit prejudice, their inflexibility, their adherence to practices that degraded women and frightened children. The psychological and social problems underlying the behaviors of my neighbors intruded upon my life through my relationship with them. If I did not oppose their racism, I was divided against myself; but if I did oppose it, I found myself isolated and berated by them. Silence in the presence of racist and sexist expressions (and I was frequently silent) meant disrespect for myself; combativeness (and that was there too), led to loss of friendly, easy ties with others. The discomfort I experienced arose because I too was enmeshed in third party influence when I communicated with my neighbors. If I did not act toward my black friends as my neighbors prescribed, I found that they tried to correct my ways by various social sanctions. If I did follow my neighbors' influence, I would have had to forego my friendly relations with my colleagues and acquaintances in the larger community. I was caught in a dissociated, confused situation. As long as third party control was dominant in this situation, there could be no truly integrated individual actions, either by me or by my neighbors, and there could be no truly mutual relations. Third party control by its very nature limits the degree of understanding and closeness that can take place between people.

Notes

1. Chauncey Starr. "Social Benefit versus Technological Risk." *Science,* 1969, Volume 165.

2. Z.F. Danes. "Water Pollution — Letter." *Science,* 1974, Volume 185.

3. Edwin B. Holt. *The Freudian Wish.* New York: Henry Holt and Co., 1915.

4. A scale of this degree of intrusiveness of a third party can be found in the book, *Motivation for Child Psychiatry Treatment,* New York: Russell and Russell, 1960. Robert Kohrman and Helen MacGregor co-authored the book with me. We referred to "space of free movement" in that work.

5. Harry Braverman. *Labor and Monopoly Capital.* New York: Monthly Review Press, 1974.

6. Philip Lichtenberg et al. *Motivation for Child Psychiatry Treatment,* op. cit.

7. Edwin B. Holt. op. cit.

CHAPTER 5

DISPOSITIONS AND THE PROCESSING OF REALITY

All of us possess an overarching outlook, a basic perspective that derives from the multitude of experiences we have had from the time of our birth. It is this assumption or conception that helps to regulate the way in which we approach each new experience. We are carriers of a most general psychic structure which is best described as a *disposition*, a predominating bent of mind or spirit. The past and future co-exist as two faces of this disposition. We remember in abstract form the totality of our past and we anticipate the future on the basis of this summarizing memory.

Conrad Aiken's short story, "Your Obituary, Well Written," captures the essence of disposition. He takes off from the extreme instance of one's imagined death, where all is past and there is no future. The narrator of the story reflects upon an advertisement he had chanced upon in which a journalist proposed: "Your obituary? Well written, reviewed by yourself, and satisfaction thus insured." Wondering what he would wish to put into his own obituary, the narrator muses:

"Mr. X. or Mr. Z., reading of me that I was an amateur archaeologist and a kind old fellow, a retired diplomatic secretary, would form no picture of me, receive from such bare bones of statement not the faintest impression of what I might call the 'essence' of my life; not the faintest. But if not these, what then? And it occurred to me suddenly that the best, and perhaps the only, way of leaving behind one a record of one's life might be, for a world of strangers, revelatory, was that of relating some single episode of one's history; some single, and if possible, central, episode in whose small prism all the colors and lights of one's soul might be seen. Seen just for a flash, and then gone. Apprehended, vividly, and then forgotten — if one ever does forget such things. And from this, I proceeded to a speculation as to just which one, of all the innumerable events of a well-filled life, I would choose as revelatory. My meeting with my wife at a ball in Calcutta, for example? Some incident of our unhappy life together — perhaps our quarrel in Venice, at the Lido? The effect of her suicide upon me, while I was dining at the Reform Club, from the P. & O. Company?... I considered all of these only to reject them — to some extent, anyway — simply because they were essentially painful. I don't know. Anyway, whatever the reasons, I did reject them, and at last found myself contemplating my odd little adventure with Reine Wilson, the novelist. Just why I fastened upon this, it would be hard to say. It was not an adventure at all; it was hardly even an episode. It was really nothing but the barest encounter, as I see it now, or as any third person would see it. If I compare it with my protracted love affair with Mrs. M., for example, or even with my very brief infatuation with Hilda K., it appears to be a mere nothing, a mere fragrance.

"A mere fragrance!... Yes, it was that; and it is for that reason, I see now, that it is so precious to me. Volatile and swift as it was, it somehow caught into itself all the scanty poetry of my life..."[1]

When Aiken's narrator refers to "some single, and if possible, central, episode in whose small prism all colors and lights of one's soul might be seen," he is alluding to the richness and intimacy of a given moment, but also to the summarization, the generalization, the global and unitary nature of our lives. When we say that a person has an optimistic temperament or that he is a sour human being, we are speaking about some system principle or general outlook on life that is part of the character of that person and is present throughout the domain of his actions. We are formulating the particular answer for that person to the question, "What about him would have to change if we were not to recognize him as the same person?" We are approximating to the nature of that psychic structure I am here calling a disposition.

A disposition is a psychic structure that has a kinship with other psychic structures such as attitude and mental set. Like attitude, a disposition is a persistent mental state of readiness. Unlike attitude, it represents a general readiness, an openness or closedness to the world. An attitude is more circumscribed because it is associated with a certain object or class of objects. A disposition is like a mental set in that it functions as a preparatory adjustment that orients a person toward certain environmental stimuli rather than others, selectively sensitizing her for apprehending them; and, similar to a mental set, it facilitates certain activities or responses rather than others. Unlike a mental set, however, a disposition is not temporary and is not caused by immediate instructions from outside.

As a psychic structure, disposition consists of the organization of the fundamental expectation of the future.

"We experience our life as something that is continuing into the future. In our thoughts, in our feelings and actions there is not only a reminiscence of past events, but also a notion that we shall exist — that is, that we shall be open to experience and shall act — in the next instant and probably in the next after that, and so on.... We have the feeling that we can make choices or decisions, and that our decisions have a real effect on our actions.... A choice refers to an anticipation of a future. The notion of a coming future involves an exptrapolation from past experiences to possible future events."[2]

The tenor of an individual's disposition depends upon the extent to which it implements equalitarian or authoritarian principles. This factor in turn is a function of how much resultant satisfaction the person has obtained in the vast array of experiences in his or her background. Great amounts of satisfaction are basic to the development of a disposition that is equalitarian; lesser amounts of total satisfaction in a person's past cause the establishment of an authoritarian perspective, and hence the focus upon exclusivity of satisfactions in relationships. A rewarding past produces the positive, equalitarian stance; a painful past generates the more negative, authoritarian one.

The equalitarian principle that is central to a disposition in which the person is open to the future derives from many experiences with full, intense, shared satisfaction. High amounts of gratification come from goals having been reached with high frequency and from equitable sharing of the fruits of such success, thus producing an expectation in the person of a high probability of success in general. This mutually inclusive sharing joined with frequency of success, which partly defines the equalitarian principle, brings to the person the general outlook so well described by Angyal,

"that the 'supplies' for one's basic needs exist in the world and that one is both adequate and worthy of obtaining these supplies."[3]

The equalitarian principle, based on mutual and equal satisfactions frequently obtained, is further defined by shared and distributed authority. Each person wants to influence others so that her particular combination of needs may be known and gratified, but each person also wants to be influenced by others so that the collective accomplishment is of a high order of complexity and integrates diverse components into entirely new forms. There is a seeking to be authoritative and a seeking to be instructed by the authority of others.

The disposition that manifests the equalitarian principles may be called confident expectation. It is a generalized expectancy that represents a summary of past experiences that provided much satisfaction, and it is continuously active as a guiding psychic structure in the present. Its basic nature is formed by the details of early life. It is nurtured by the mutual gratifications that the infant and young child shared with her parents, but it continues to grow and to influence a person's life throughout the years.

Therese Benedek has developed the notion of what I have called confident expectation under the term "confidence," and she has traced its theoretical linkage within psychoanalytic thought:

"Confidence is used as a term to designate an emotional state of the infant which has developed through multiple repetitions of the gratifying experiences of symbiosis. The concept implies an ego organization in which the effects of the libidinal relationship with the mother through introjection have become a part of the mental organization of the child.... Both confidence and hope are qualities of ego organization which enable the infant (and the adult as well) to span an unpleasant situation in the present and project the expectation of gratification into the future."[4]

GETTING EVEN

One property of this disposition of confident expectation merits immediate clarification. A psychic structure is not the same thing as a conscious awareness; the psyche and consciousness are different matters. A person who possesses a confident expectation is not always consciously confident, hopeful or trusting. A person may be very uncertain about what will happen in any new encounter and indeed may consciously be anxious, diffident and apprehensive. However, he is guided in his processing of the event and the regulation of his actions by the underlying confident expectation. It would be misleading to equate the orienting disposition, which in this case is confident, with the momentary awareness. Burgers expresses the same idea:

> "It is advisable not to tie the notion of expectation or anticipation to consciousness, but to assume it is located (insofar as we may use this word) at a 'deeper level.' Evidently in humans it often reaches consciousness, but probably even here this is not always the case."[5]

An authoritarian orientation can also be manifested in a disposition. Authoritarianism is based on two (faulty) assumptions: (1) that transactions between people eventuate in unequal satisfactions for the participants, and (2) that authority is used to gather the greater proportion of satisfactions to oneself while resistance to authority is used to protect one's share of the rewards of events. The assumption inherent in authoritarianism is that there is mutual exclusivity in social relations, and patterns of dominance-submission are played out continually.

I have called the disposition that expresses the authoritarian principle *essential ambivalent anticipation*.[6] A guiding psychic structure, it is a generalized expectancy that represents a summary of past experiences that provided gratifications heavily mixed with frustrations. Its basic nature, like that of confident expectation, is shaped by the concrete circumstances of early life. For example, the infant and young child may have experienced much of her mother's anxiety or annoyance when she was nursing, and thus taken in with her mother's milk the sense that all pleasure is contaminated with pain; and she may have sensed simultaneously that social relations are exclusive in that her pleasure was obtained at her mother's expense and, conversely, mother's joy was her sorrow.

Mutual exclusiveness and inequality of satisfactions comprise the central defining factor that is associated with resultant contradictory and low gratification. In the many encounters that make up early life, the child may have had predominantly competitive social relations which produce a relatively lower total gratification quotient. Consequently, she develops an essential ambivalent anticipation. She may develop such a disposition even if her parents are self-denying rather than dominating or if she comes from a wealthy heritage rather than an impoverished one. Whether the person is the presumed more favored one or the less favored one, she is engaged in relations that roughly balance pleasures and unpleasures, thus creating the basic anticipation of an ambivalent, approach-avoidance, push-pull type.

Confident expectation and essential ambivalent anticipation are polar dispositions that define a dimension. At the upper extreme, confident expectation, a psychic structure is developed and held that is associated with a history of much satisfaction and is burdened with little dissatisfaction. At the lower extreme of this dimension, essential ambivalent anticipation, the psychic structure is founded upon an equal mixture of satisfactions and dissatisfactions in the organized whole that constitutes a disposition. Individuals would not survive infancy if they did not experience more fulfillment than pain. Although in the midst of agony we often believe that our suffering is greater than our gain, we could not maintain the integrity of our organism as a system were unpleasure to outweigh the positive meeting of needs.

The dimension bounded by the two dispositions does not and cannot reach from one hundred percent pleasure in the ideal confident expectation, and fifty percent pleasure–fifty percent unpleasure in the pure form of essential ambivalent anticipation. No one alive is close to these absolute possibilities.

Within the context of a confident expectation, differences between persons, obstacles to achievement, and delays in gratification are understood as necessary and useful components of complexity in effort and profundity in pleasure. Life is seen as challenge and struggle with mostly positive resolutions. Within the contrasting perspective of essential ambivalent anticipation the differences that exist between people are interpreted as ominous. Strangers or members of outgroups are likely to cause personal difficulty and are viewed with suspicion. Obstacles and delays are seen as asssuring a high ratio of dissatisfaction relative to satisfaction. Life is seen as a bitter endeavor to eke out more pleasure than the minimum that is expected.

Persons who bear the authoritarian disposition manifest the mistrust and hopelessness that derives from the contradictoriness of their experience. Because they have an essential ambivalent anticipation, they allow the least awareness of consciousness of that ambivalence. The concept of intolerance of ambivalence or ambiguity developed by the authors of *The Authoritarian Personality*[7] is relevant here. Persons who are authoritarian possess deep ambivalence toward their parents, peers, subordinates and authorities, but they are intolerant of the complexity necessary to feel at one time both sides of the ambivalence. So they idealize some figures, on the one hand, and exaggerate the faults of other figures, on the other hand.

Persons of an equalitarian nature are capable of allowing themselves to be openly ambivalent and are therefore less fragmented. Because they *experience* more contradictions, they engage in fewer divisive, exclusive, splitting relations. Those of us who appear superficially to be most torn apart are frequently more unified and intergrated than those of us who pretend to singularity of feeling.

Thus, individuals with confident expectations differ markedly from individuals with essential ambivalent anticipations by the amount of gratification they have known. But, they differ in their present functioning as well. We need only look at their ideologies, their social and political orientations, their artistic activities, their attitudes toward child rearing, even their mental health to realize the scope of influence of these dispositions.

From the nature of their dispositions, some more than other circumstances, ideas, social positions and political thoughts are

familiar and readily understood by different individuals.

Is it not remarkable that most of us have available immediate answers for solving the most intricate and complex social and political problems? As soon as some problem is defined, whether it be crime in the streets, unwed motherhood, the need for public welfare, unemployment, disarray in schools, or a revolution in Latin America, arguments are immediately forthcoming that presume to explain the problems and to suggest solutions. We reach these conclusions so rapidly because they are based in significant degree upon our pre-established perspective, that is, through our essential ambivalent anticipation or confident expectation rather than upon devotion to the study of the intricacies of reality. On the basis of past experience, each of us is primed to process and assimilate stimuli from our world either more or less rigidly, and we are differently primed in the sense that certain phenomena attract our interest and involvement more easily than others.

Thus, those of us whose developmental history has been filled with conflict and frustration, such that we operate by the authoritarian principle, are prepared to understand immediately the following social positions:

- Criminals merit severe punishment.
- Military power for all possible exigencies imaginable is necessary for national security.
- Automation is inherently destructive of human welfare.
- Mothers on welfare who have illegitimate children are promiscuous or have such children to increase their benefits.
- People are selfish; it is human nature to want to dominate others in one's own private interest.

Conversely, those among us with the trust and hope inherent in the confident expectation resonate to the following alternate social postures:

- Crimes are signs or symptoms of underlying causative factors. Understanding of the particular causes will provide guidance for social action in given instances.
- Military power must be geared to clear and probable threats continuously monitored, not to every conceivable danger.
- Automation can be used collectively either in modes that are productive or in modes that are destructive of human welfare. We must decide together how to use the processes we have created.
- Mothers on welfare who have illegitimate children are probably burdened individuals.
- People serve their own needs when productively and mutually engaged with others.

The first point to be made, therefore, is that we are prejudiced by our dispositions toward various points of view according to the hopefulness or hopelessness, trust or mistrust, that is characteristic of them. We are all biased. To be objective is not to be without bias because by the very presence of general expectations we are all more ready to receive certain ideas and facts than we are to receive others. We resonate one to another or differ one from another by the substance of these dispositions and the ideological positions to which they take us.[8]

We can understand a dismal historical fact by this conceptual analysis. It has been consistently true over many generations that most poor, oppressed, defeated individuals, for longer or shorter periods of time, support and defend social and political leaders who develop policies and programs that impoverish, oppress and defeat them. Part of their support must be attributed to the actual repressive forces instituted by such leaders, but another part stems from the personality structures of the downtrodden. Why should the most harried individuals ever support dictators or presidents who do not serve their interests? And why with such dedication and passion in their allegiance? Why do the children of the oppressed fill the ranks of the police and the military in exploitative regimes? They are supportive, I believe, because those leaders are the spokesmen for policies based on firm attitudes of mistrust and hopelessness, the characteristics that define the essential ambivalent anticipation which are held by persons whose lives have caused them to be excessively exploited. For example, such leaders often offer "hopes" if their followers will simply rely upon them for magical solutions, as if the social problems are not complex system properties with historical and current social determinants. These leaders promise much, pretend to be "responsible," and accomplish little, yet their followers continue to believe in them. Persons who are oppressed "understand" such exploitative leaders precisely because they share with them common authoritarian dispositions.

The major social policies and forms of organization of society have a direct impact upon us because they connect with our dispositions.

Each individual within a society is affected by the systemic principles of that society, of government and other social institutions. For example, any government establishes its priorities as it administers the affairs of society, priorities that embody themes of a very broad scope. As a goverment gives shape to general policies, it ranks defence expenditures and health expenditures, or measures the needs of producers and consumers relative to each other. The result of these allocations determine a government's character, its organizing principles or thematic structure. While all governments deal with many different areas of human concern, each government articulates the manner in which these areas are related to each other and the posture with which the separate areas are addressed. Governments are systems and have organizing principles.

The systemic principles of a government are perceived by individuals who react to them according to their dispositions. The general perspective of the larger system, government, and the general outlook of the smaller system, the individual, are connected so that the individual is *directly* moved by the character of his government. When a government radiates optimism in its plans and priorities, it affects citizens according to their confident expectation or essential ambivalent anticipation, confirming hope, disconfirming suspicion. People are encouraged by this influence to act in a more open way, to behave freely, or, at least, to mute their mistrust while waiting to see what transpires in the society.

When a society becomes authoritarian, it too affects everyone, but it affects most profoundly those persons who hold an essential ambivalent anticipation. By its preoccupations and organization, such a society supports persons with dispositions that contain hopelessness and mistrust and challenges persons with dispositions that are hopeful and trusting. The society greets those persons who already suffer from their difficult assumptions with a verification of these negative assumptions that further prevents them from developing into a more positive orientation, while it only raises temporary obstacles or even challenges to those persons with sufficient confidence to resist the idea that a poor, sick, competitive and destructive society is necessary.

We not only hold contradictory ideas and create actions with contradictory demands in them; we are also committed to these contradictions and invested in their appearance according to the degree of essential ambivalent anticipation dominating our basic assumption.

A disposition, whether confident expectation or essential ambivalent anticipation, may be seen as a gestalt that is derived from many experiences. It is a registration of successes and failures, honors and dishonors, promises kept or ignored in social relations, a general sense of the probabilities that goals will be attained and whether people are to be trusted. The gestalt is formed from two probability patterns. First, there is the frequency of success and trustworthiness over all experiences lived, a probability over many events. If I have had a host of events today, arising, breakfast, a conversation with my son, an encounter in the bookshop, a letter to a friend..., I can note that a certain proportion of these events meet an acceptable level of gratification. I thus register that percentage as a frequency of trusting successes. When I multiply this by all the events that have constituted my life, I have a huge base on which my disposition is grounded. But, in addition to having multitudes of experiences in a lifetime from which to generate a probability, I have the internal nature of each single experience as well. No one experience is all gratification; no given other person is completely attuned to me. Thus, each event is more or less successful, more or less filled with open, honorable, responsible relations with others. Probabilities flow from the internal qualities of each event too. In other words, one particular happening fits two-third of my needs, but directly punishes me in other ways. Another event is a mildly pleasing moment, one which satisfies a good number of desires mildly and frustrates few of them. The single event has proportions of success and suspicion that are translatable into probability or disposition.

The person who has an essential ambivalent anticipation expects that more of any event is going to be difficult and unpleasant, and he knows that any happening in which he functions will have a strong mixture of pain with pleasure. Working from this assumption, he tends to put many contradictions into his actions. What has been true in his past is therefore assumed to be true for the future. If an encounter comes along that does not have the expected discomfort, often he will unconsciously add trouble to it so that he can be with the familiar blend; for instance, when he has a truly pleasurable moment, he will become suspicious that something will arise to spoil it, and his worry itself will be an encroachment upon the purity of the pleasure. The gestalt that defines the disposition of essential ambivalent anticipation needs internal contradictions to maintain its probability form; and people live and act on the basis of this disposition more fundamentally than they live according to the particular probabilities of any moment in time. People hold contradictory attitudes primarily as these attitudes are part of the larger, global expectation.

Consequently, when we try to combat contradictory ideas or distortions of the truth, we are often unsuccessful because we direct our arguments to the elements and not to the total anticipation. By speaking to the particularities, we approach one component but cannot deal with its contradictory companion. For the persons whose minds we would change, however, these individual elements assume meaning only as they fulfill the requirements of the generalized form. While we direct ourselves to one portion of satisfaction, they are attending to the whole. So it is that people who are intolerant of ambiguity are difficult to reason with. While they are often avid for surface consistency — given their intolerance of ambivalence — they cannot believe in deep or full consistency because the basis of their general anticipations requires the existence of contradictoriness. They want to appear consistent because they cannot bear open realization of their own ambivalence, but they invariably introduce inconsistency into arguments. The more they are given rationales, the more obstinate they become in defence of their flawed assumptions about life. One must reach them first by means of some contact with their dispositions, contradictions and all, rather than by way of logic and reasoning about particulars.

A very direct illustration of this point puzzled me when I first worked in a child guidance clinic. A number of parents would tell us after we had completed diagnostic sessions and explained to them the need for treatment that they understood what was required, believed us when we said the symptoms that brought the child to the clinic could be alleviated, and respected our therapeutic capacities. So far, so good. But, despite our assurance, these parents were convinced that successful treatment would do no good! Most of these parents kept their children and themselves from the treatment program not because they feared the program would fail, but because it would succeed and yet make no difference. Since they "knew" that every positive gain is balanced by loss, that is, since they judged a long-run effort by their essential ambivalent anticipations, they imputed contradictions to the process and outcome and refused to pursue something organized to produce greater happiness in their lives. No rational discussion could persuade them that the future would differ from their expectation.

A different example of the point that people with essential ambivalent anticipations expect and need contradictions comes from the experiences of prejudice. Everyone who has been discriminated against for being black, Jewish, a woman or poor, is familiar with the assurance given by the most prejudiced person: "Some of my best friends are" black Jewish, women or poor. Prejudiced individuals do not see the contradiction between treating all members of a class according to a stereotype different from that which they apply to one or several members of that class. If some of their friends are members of that class, then they must be individualizing those persons while they perceive all others in that grouping by cliches. Prejudiced people seldom respond to reasoning on this issue because the contradictoriness is normal and necessary to their general orienting anticipation.

Although we are all biased or predisposed, we are not equally closed to reality. Some biases foreclose options or predetermine outcomes more than other biases. Some dispositions are more open-ended than others.

Confident expectation differs in its predisposing qualities from essential ambivalent anticipation. The hopeful-trusting disposition leads to further contact with reality, to increased specification or articulation of that reality. A confident expectation enables the person to seek the novel in the present moment, to create new conditions of engagement, to explore alternatives, to sift among the positives and negatives around her. Such an expectation encourages its possessor not to imagine in panglossian manner the necessary arrival of the best in the world, but to act on the assumption that good and fruitful deeds can be brought into play if reality is closely observed and wisely acted upon.

The mistrustful orientation leads to more rapid and self-enforced limitation upon encounters with reality. When a person enters a new situation with a general sense of hopelessness or mistrust, he is biased toward a quick, stereotyped, pain-centered processing of reality. The underlying thrust is to search reality for minimum clues about what is familiar from the past and what is most dangerous and fraught with peril. From these cues an action is constructed which is relatively immune to new inputs and dynamically changing meaning. Once the assessment has been developed and the action settled upon, newness and diversity are shunned.

Barbara Tuchman in *The Guns of August* has drawn a similar picture of human processing of reality in her reference to the activities of the generals in the opening days of World War I.

"He [General Lanrezac] did not know their names or numbers but he knew they were there. He knew or deducted from reconnaissance that greater numbers were coming at him than he could dispose of. Evaluation of enemy strength is not an absolute, but a matter of piecing together scraps of reconnaissance and intelligence to form a picture, if possible, a picture to fit preconceived theories or to suit the demands of a particular strategy. What a staff makes out of the available evidence depends upon the degree of optimism or pessimism among them, on what they want to believe or fear to believe, and somtimes upon the sensitivity or intuition of an individual."[9]

Mrs. Tuchman argues that the General, like almost all leading military men, was of a pessimistic bent and this essential ambivalent anticipation caused him to distort the information he received. The consequence was that he feared the worst when he could reasonably have inferred the best, and he lost the chance for a quick and relatively easy victory.

Nathan Isaacs, in discussing intelllectual growth of young children talks about the "why" questions that children pose. He asks us to stop and consider the function and value of the readily observed fact that children are constantly asking "why" about things and events in the world. "Why are you sad, Mommy?" "Why can't I play with the knife?" Why does the sun go away?" In consideration of this fact, Isaacs writes:

"The general position is that we carry about with us beliefs or assumptions of all degrees of fixity, and that our 'why' questions testify with varying degrees of force, both to their strength of lodgment (at the time), and to their liability to a greater or less measure of dislodgment.... Our absolutely fixed and innate assumptions probably do not come into the open. When any do so, they have presumably begun to get unmoored.... Those that do come into the open, however, as definite established assumptions, may offer greater or less resistance to change, in the child as in the adult."

The role of adults in helping to establish the general expectations and anticipations held by the child is also addressed by Isaacs. In the following passage he refers to a "standard of explanation" which I would translate into a cognitive or intellectual form of confident expectation or essential ambivalent anticipation.

"The adults round the child determine progressively his *standard* of explanation (i.e., of what is attainable or considered valid and satisfactory as explanation); and this standard will more and more determine when he will be puzzled, how he will then try to readjust or extend his assumptions or beliefs or knowledge, what knowledge or insight he will think possible or desirable, and when and how he will be satisfied.

"But these are factors that will beyond anything else decide the general character and level of his intellectual life. They will determine the degree of control which actuality is allowed to exercise over his notions and beliefs. Nothing can be more fatal to growth in adequate knowledge, or in the capacity for objective judgment, than the vitiation of that actuality - control by a low social standard of explanation."[10]

Many reformers in the past have neglected this aspect of the functioning of people when they proposed that education, by providing a series of benevolent experiences for children, could rather easily and directly cancel the negative effects of earlier life activities. They believed that if we could educate our entire population, we could overcome crime and war and unemployment. They found, to their dismay, that the children who were most ready to pick up the benefits of education were not the most disheartened, but the most happy; not the oppressed, but the well off. It became clear that something within the children intervened to prevent them from making full use of the opportunities before them.

When some societal leaders propose that capital punishment acts as a deterrent, they presume, among other things, that persons who might commit capital crimes will hear the specificity of their communication. Such potential criminals will learn that he who murders shall be severely punished. The people who hear the details of this message, however, are the individuals who can allow the particulars of the world to make themselves known because they hold a confident expectation. These persons are the very human beings least likely to believe, even momentarily, that attacking and demolishing another human being will solve problems. (Though we all have murder in our hearts at one time or another.) Unfortunately, the persons toward whom the deterrent message is beamed, those with an essential ambivalent anticipation, hear something very different from what it is intended that they should hear. They perceive the general content (e.g., prisons have electric chairs), rather than the discriminatory one (e.g., murderers are electrocuted), and they learn one more time that the world is a hostile place where the massive powers of society are organized by the principle that one kills and is killed. The aim of deterring cannot work properly, therefore, because the ingredients intended to deter cannot be communicated to the right people. Whatever other reasons account for the failure of capital punishment as a deterrent, this one must be added to the list.

The essence of child-rearing is the fostering of hope and trust. Training children in regard to specific behaviors is of secondary importance.

The appropriate way to socialize a child according to the perspective developed here is to provide her with a multitude of joy and satisfactions so that she will assume the world is good, goals can be reached, people can be trusted, in other words, so that she will develop a confident expectation. With this psychic structure, the child can discover and create a wide range of actions as she deals directly with reality, and she can adapt these many actions to the requirements of her life.

This view is in opposition to everyday child development theory, and to a considerable portion of scientific theory, which suggests that by means of direct training children acquire socially appropriate ways of behaving. This point of view suggests that children learn, often by mere imitation or direct identification, to take roles, to behave with manners, to learn obedience to the laws and customs of society so that when they become adults they will know how to act. But it is faulty to suspect that nature asks a parent to predict the future of his society so precisely that he can prepare his child for it by some kind of conditioning; and it is more constricting upon human nature than necessary to require that a person live his daily life by merely repeating what he has learned in the past. The problem for children is to learn how to take in reality and to discover their own needs, and how to construct new forms of relationships. It is not to learn what specific behaviors are right.

Three levels of severity of psychopathology represent different degrees of confident expectation and essential ambivalent anticipation in persons' dispositions.

While not commonly acknowledged in technical circles, there are obvious and definite degrees of psychopathology that are of quantitative as well as qualitative difference. In an earlier publication on depression,[11] which has served as background to this present essay, I considered three principles or orientations of expectancy; and I suggested three levels of depression that could be determined according to which of these orientations were predominant. The three orientations concern: (1) an expectancy associated with a particular situation; (2) an expectancy associated with behavior styles; and (3) an expectancy associated with a generalized goal (i.e., one's disposition, whether tilted toward full confident expectation or toward essential ambivalent anticipation).

The characteristic behavior of persons who are neurotic (least severely disturbed) contains problems in the area of expectancy associated with a particular situation. Behavior of persons who are psychotic (most severely disturbed) is shaped conspicuously by failures in basic trust or basic confidence, that is, by an essential ambivalent anticipation. Between neurosis and psychosis is another layer of disturbance, unfortunately lacking in a single name. Persons labeled as borderline, character disorders, personality disorders, psychopaths, schizoids, alcoholic or other drug abusers, function at this level of disturbance. Alcoholism and sociopathy, for instance, tend to be forms of depression that are more severe than most neuroses and less severe than most psychoses. Behavior of persons living with these middle-level problems is affected clearly by expectancies associated with behavior styles.

The neurotic is a person, then, who starts with an assumption that life in general is adequate. He has a variety of styles of action in his repertory so that he can use different styles in different circumstances. He tends to stumble in coordinating the particularities of the present. Neurotic individuals have special problems that are focused on arranging all of the discrete elements in a given situation.

Persons with character disorders (psychopathy, etc.) assume generally that there is considerable cost for any gain. Accordingly, they focus upon the few or narrow styles of action that have assured them of enough satisfaction in the past for them to persist in living. They tend to see each experience in term of the styles of action they accept as appropriate for the circumstance. They rely on rigid patterns, conventions, habits, ploys, games, or interpersonal stunts. When trouble arises, they fall back on the addictions, rituals, obsessions or repetitions that characterize their pathology.

The psychotic is a person who starts from the position that the world is hostile and ungiving and who applies his general view to his styles and momentary behavior. His expectancies about the specifics of the present are dictated by his basic hopelessness and mistrust. Consequently, he tends to lack enriched information about the present, to rely instead upon pale and old versions of the realities around him. The omnipresence of his essential ambivalent anticipation deeply colors his actions. Psychotic individuals confront each here and now as if it were the eternal world itself, as if each single thing were everything.

If people differ according to which of these expectancies is dominant in their lives, they are similar in that for every event in their lives all three guiding principles come into play. Each of us approaches a new situation in our lives first according to our basic disposition, either our confident expectation or essential ambivalent anticipation; a new event brings us face to face with the totality of our lives and of the world around us. Insofar as the new circumstance contains unkowns, we rely on this general perspective to fill the gaps. On the basis of this perspective, we next try styles of action that narrow the world and make it more manageable. These styles of action are formed by the disposition and by the information coming to us about this specific form of the universe that constitutes our present. Finally, on the basis of both a general expectancy and an expectancy associated with the behavior styles, we put our needs and those forces active outside us together to meet the particularities of any situation.

The unique co-exists with the universal, and the most adequate portrayal of a special instance portrays also our most general being. Because every moment of our lives is different in its details from every other moment, each is unique and special. We seldom have the same combination of needs and desires impelling us to act, and even when our motives approximate an earlier pattern, we do not have the same social and material forces with which to connect them. We thus have opportunities for great creativity in the fashioning of our life experience as a consequence of the inner and outer variations in forces that we must reconcile.

Yet at each moment our dispositions are guiding us. The most general, the most universal aspect of our being directs our each and every action. The creativity we manage to instill in our behavior is a function of the disposition as well as the many forces operating within and upon us. Right now is, in some sense, forever. (Those of us who are not psychotic also function on this most general level, but with a more hopeful and trusting disposition that allows us to also attend to details of the present in their own possibility.)

When we respond to others, we reverse the path of our own construction of events. Where we move from dispositions to styles to particular forms of behavior, we react to concrete, unique behavior of others and are responding to the general, the underlying disposition, behind that behavior. When someone presents to us something that carries through her disposition in genuine expression, she moves the deepest part of our own personality in resonance. The creativity of other people awakens deep expectations in us. William Empson remarks on this in respect to poetry:

"There is always in great poetry a feeling of generalization from a case which has been presented definitely; there is always an appeal to a background of human experience which is all the more present when it cannot be named.... What I would suppose is that, whenever a receiver of poetry is moved by an apparently simple line, what are moving in him are the traces of a great part in his past experience and the structure of his past judgments."[12]

Carl Jung makes almost the same point:

"The secret of artistic creation and of the effectiveness of art is to be found in a return to the state of *participation mystique* — to that level of experience at which it is man who lives and not the individual, and at which the weal or woe of the single human being does not count, but only human existence. This is why every great work of art is objective and impersonal, but nonetheless profoundly moves us each and all."[13]

From this survey we can sense the tremendous influence that dispositions have in our everyday dealings. They affect what we fear and hope, how we act, the nature of our interpretations of what others are doing, the standards of judgments we deem reasonable, the level of disturbance we are likely to reach when things are too difficult for us to master, and our social-political stances in the world. Perhaps, because our culture has elevated reason and rationality to such heights, we have lost contact with this pre-rational phenomenon. From not sufficiently taking disposition into account we have been limited in the work we do. Appropriate social planning and effective social struggle, the ability to mobilize people and institutions, require that we understand the meaning that dispositions carry in individuals and that we reckon with their influence.

Notes

1. Conrad Aiken. "Your Obituary, Well Written." In: *The Short Stories of Conrad Aiken.* New York: Duell, Sloan and Pearce, 1950.

2. J.M. Burgers. "Casuality and Anticipation." *Science,* 1975. Volume 189.

3. Andras Angyal. *Neurosis and Treatment: A Holistic Theory.* New York: Wiley, 1965.

4. Therese Benedek. *Psychoanalytic Investigations.* New York: Quadrangle, 1973. Benedek relates her construct of "confidence" to conceptions developed by other writers: Balint's "primary object love;" Ferenczi's "primary narcissistic omnipotence," which was the conception that influenced me most significantly in my early work; Abraham's "oral libidinal satisfaction;" Erikson's "basic trust." I would add Angyal's "healthy gestalt" to her list.

5. J.M. Burgers. op. cit.

6. This may be the point at which it is appropriate to note the relation of the authoritarian principle and its expression in the essential ambivalent anticipation to the set of ideas developed in the classic, *The Authoritarian Personality,* by T.W. Adorno, Else Frenkel-Brunswik, Daniel J. Levinson and Nevitt Sanford. New York: Harper & Brothers, 1950. I have been considerably influenced by this work. Indeed, I was a graduate student working with one of its authors (D.J. Levinson) when the book appeared and I wrote a master's thesis under his direction on *Authoritarian Personality and Religious Ideology: An Analysis of Standardized Personal Documents of High and Low Scorers on the Religious Conventionalism Scale.* Cleveland, Ohio: Case Western Reserve University Library, 1950. There is much overlap in these ideas, most evidenced, I think, in the analysis of the intolerance of ambivalence and attitudes toward authority. The difference is this: I have kept to a strict and narrow definition of authoritarianism and of disposition and have derived all else from these; their work has been more inclusive and has involved many more, somewhat loosely intergrated, concepts.

7. T.W. Adorno et al. op. cit.

8. For a related analysis, "ideo-affective resonance," see Silvan

GETTING EVEN

Tomkins, "Left and Right: A Basic Dimension of Ideology and Personality." In: *The Study of Lives,* Robert W. White, Editor. New York: Atherton, 1963.

9. Barbara Tuchman. *The Guns of August.* New York: Dell, 1963.

10. Nathan Isaacs. "Appendix A: Children's 'Why' Questions." In: *Intellectual Growth of Young Children,* Susan Isaacs. New York: Harcourt, Brace, 1930.

11. Philip Lichtenberg. "A Definition and Analysis of Depression." *A.M.A. Archives of Neurology and Psychiatry,* 1957, Volume 77.

12. William Empson. *Seven Types of Ambiguity.* New York: Meridian, 1955.

13. Carl G. Jung. *Psychological Types.* New York: Harcourt, Brace 1926.

CHAPTER 6

ON RESPONSIBILITY

I

In the decades of the 1960s and 1970s demands arose from students, activists and representatives of the poor seeking new power and participatory democracy. The demands were appealing and yet inadequate at the same time. The idea of people actively participating in establishing policy and regulating leadership on a systematic basis is appealing because it leads to increased creativity and spontaneity in social institutions. Added openness, challenge and uncertainty produce an increase in the diversity of perspectives, a kind of dynamic and productive interplay of forces.

But there was also a faulty conception that accompanied these demands for new power and greater participation which distorted this positive democratizing movement and contributed to its fading from the social scene. Those activists and students who insisted on the necessity of developing new forms often seemed to be asserting that all hierarchies are inherently authoritarian; and they indicated that the only real choice was between complete absence of hierarchy or hierarchy that is autocratic; between chaos and structure; between every person as all things or every person as an alienated specialist. They were wrong. The truth is that order, structure and hierarchy are fundamental to personal and social existence. All collections of people find ways to organize themselves; even those who denounce hierarchy sooner or later come to rely upon some degree of structure in order to work together and to reach a goal. When the students and activists practiced this fact, they felt disloyal and retreated from the field of social struggle or gave up the idea of full participatory democracy.

Recognition of the value of structure, the division of labor and vertical organization does not necessarily signify enthronement of arbitrary authority. Authoritarianism and hierarchical structure are not the same thing; and it is confusing, and ultimately demoralizing, to suggest that they are. This simple reality means that the true choice we must make in respect to our institutions and our society as a whole is between equalitarian hierarchical systems and authoritarian hierarchical systems. The key to distinguishing between equalitarian and authoritarian hierarchies, I believe, lies in understanding the way in which responsibility is defined and allocated. When we discover how different interpretations of responsibility are played out, we also find authoritarianism or equalitarianism dominating the structure according to which meaning of responsibility is ascendant.

II

A major impetus for this study in responsibility and hierarchy came from investigations into the personality characteristics of public welfare clients.[1] These people are continually subjected to stresses imposed by bureaucratic, hierarchical structures in organizations and by autocratic authorities who control resources that they desperately need. Although most of us in society are frequently confronted with stressful situations — more than we customarily acknowledge, I suspect — it is also true that most of us find ways to be on the superior side in hierarchical arrangements for some more or less large segments of our time after we leave childhood behind. Most of us develop methods for accommodating to hierarchies containing arbitrary authority without ruffling the system in frequent, direct confrontations. Unlike welfare clients, we do not regularly and unwittingly upset the bureaucrats, fight the autocrats, passively and indirectly defy benevolent authorities, or defer to others and then ignore the commitments exacted from our deference. In strange and remarkable ways these clients have created and developed techniques that do just these things.

These clients exist on the underside in many authoritarian hierarchical relationships. They must consume hours of their daily activities in dealing with landlords, medical clinics, employment agencies, church officers, police officers, and bosses at work; and the superiors with whom they must contend are among the most petty, most despotic persons in the society. The authorities that welfare clients deal with are themselves entwined in superior-inferior relationships of an autocratic nature so that much of their time is also spent on the underside. These authorities then jealously guard and insist upon their superior position whenever they are in a position to enjoy this status. The troubles with authoritarian hierarchy are not limited to the fact of oppression levied upon the subjects within authoritarian structures; authority itself is debased and distorted.

Authoritarian hierarchical systems are a prominent factor in the lives of clients who receive help from public welfare programs. It is also true that these individuals have major problems in respect to responsibility. These clients are commonly thought to be highly irresponsible. Indeed, frequently cited are instances of husbands deserting their wives; families failing to pay their rent, their telephone bills, their electric bills; money being spent on "nonessentials" like television sets or automobiles; and children's difficulties in school remaining unattended. Many clients overlook or avoid appointments with prospective employers, with doctors and dentists, with their welfare caseworkers, often having asserted previously that they fully desire and intend to honor these commitments. Caseworkers frequently find themselves badgering these clients into promises ("Yes, I will go to the employment office, the eye doctor, the district attorney, the hospital to get my child's birth certificate, the psychiatric clinic...."), only to learn at a later date that these promises have been unfulfilled ("I was sick, I forgot, I had a headache, I had something else to do, my mother could not baby-sit, I went but it was closed....")

It also became apparent to us that the worst abuses in the administration of welfare services stem from forcible efforts to make these clients responsible in one way or another. People are abruptly separated from assistance if they fail to meet obligations placed upon them by the caseworker or the system. If a woman does not go to the district attorney to have him locate her missing husband and bring the fellow into court, she is not mailed her welfare check. Midnight raids conducted by zealous welfare investigators, aimed at exposing the presence of a man in the house who can be made to support the woman and her children, have no other justification than holding responsible these presumably exploitative women on welfare. Under the self-righteous pronouncements that they are enforcing the moral codes of the community, administrators arbitrarily cut from the rolls of public assistance women who have newly-born illegitimate children.

Starting with these general observations, my co-workers and I refined further our analysis of the sense of responsibility. The first thing we learned was paradoxical: *the clients produce the outcomes of apparent irresponsibility through an exaggerated sense of responsibility.* That is to say, the aim of the clients is to assure that they will be responsible for the events in their lives. Because these people feel so powerless in all facets of their lives, their need for control over situations pre-empts other considerations. Thus, they strive for such dominance even in circumstances where power rightfully belongs to other people and when their behavior is self-defeating. The clients find that circumstances oppose rather than respond favorably to their efforts most of the time.

As we began to study these clients and their use of authority in more depth, we discovered that *responsibility is composed of two fundamental elements, primacy and accountability.* The primacy component pertains to such matters as initiative, leadership, dominance and innovation. In every distinct human transaction one person or group becomes the primary agent or casual force in the transaction; someone is "responsible for" the conditions that give boundaries and structure to the transaction. That person is frequently associated with the beginnings of the episode, the determination of the central goal of the episode, and the ending of it. In summary, the one who has primacy in the interaction possesses the initiative. To say that she is primary does not mean that she can take a greater amount of satisfaction from the transaction than any other person can. Sometimes we confuse this issue and think that attaining primacy in a relationship is identical with aggrandizement and exploitation. However, this is a false assumption. To have primacy, to assert initiative, to be the primary agent is not the same as to collect a greater share of the rewards in the relationship.

Accountability, the second element in responsibility, pertains to control over exploitation, that is, it touches upon the means by which equality of satisfaction is invoked by the collaborating members. Accountability fits into the network of issues that includes trust, fair play, social interest and social consciousness. If primacy entails being "responsible for" an event, accountability concerns being "responsible to" others for coordination of effort and for the equitable distribution of satisfactions. For example, when we hold a criminal responsible for his acts, we are emphasizing his accountability to society. Similarly, a major problem in large social systems is to hold leaders accountable for their decisions. We call a person accountable who has carried through to completion the obligations to others that he has assumed.

Different interpretations of responsibility depend upon the way in which primacy and accountability are interrelated. Responsibility is open to ambiguous interpretation because these elements may be seen either to operate in unison or to function independently of each other. The interplay between the two produces three definitions of responsibility.

(1) **Responsibility is equated with a balance of primacy and accountability.**

As a person acquires increasing primacy, he also becomes increasingly answerable to those affected by his initiative; in addition, as a person takes on increasing accountability, he is given increasing power of initiative. This first definition of responsibility, in which primacy and accountability are balanced, is basic to equalitarianism. It is assumed that the one who is in the primacy position will also be answerable for his actions to those who are in the relationship with him. When primacy and accountability are balanced, a person allows another to take precedence in the shaping of an encounter providing that he also accepts an accountability — an accountability that insures recognition of the rights of all persons involved in the transaction. Similarly, if a person is subjected to the primacy of another through the social role of that other, he will strain to make accountable the person upon whose primacy he depends. By attaching accountability to the acceptance of initiative, individuals act to assure equality in personal relationships.

(2) **Responsibility is connected solely with primacy as cause of events.**

To be responsible, according to this definition, means to possess initiative, to command circumstances so that they follow from the interests of the individual who is considered responsible. This definition is connected with authoritarianism. Within this conception of responsibility the issue of accountability is more or less ignored. At one extreme within this type, a person may consider answerability as totally irrelevant to responsibility; at the other extreme, the person is ready to become accountable as soon as her primacy is established.

This focus upon primacy to the exclusion of accountability is the sense of responsibility we found quite typical of clients in public assistance agencies. A client comes to a welfare agency assuming that the public servants she meets will measure what they can offer against her needs as she presents them. The person finds instead that she must provide assurance that she merits help; she is required to demonstrate trustworthiness, a readiness to be held accountable. Given that her personality style is geared to the entrenchment of her own control over the events in her life, she cannot allow for her accountability until after she has established her own primacy. Thus, the client is faced with a contradiction and the relationship with the caseworker is turbulent and frustrating. Those few caseworkers who are aware of this personality trait often adjust to it by making certain that clients know their needs are put first. This invariably produces more effective transactions.

(3) **Responsibility is connected solely with answerability.**

By this definition, to be responsible means to fulfill obligations, to render account for one's actions or decisions, to demonstrate loyalty to a set of norms or to one's superiors, to accommodate to the requirements of an organization, group or society. This definition is also associated with authoritarianism. Within this idea of responsibility are variations in the degree to which primacy is overlooked or dismissed. At the furthest limit in this conception of responsibility, a person may consider primacy to be extraneous to any sense of responsibility. Loyalty, obedience, carrying out obligations, abiding by laws and mores, partiotism, each for its own sake, constitute expressions of this sense of responsibility in the extreme. In the less extreme case a person allows primacy to others as soon as their accountability is assured. In other words, answerability is the prerequisite to primacy. I have already suggested that caseworkers adopt this definition of responsibility in their work with clients in public welfare agencies. The belief that clients are irresponsible also stems from this view: because clients refuse to be answerable prior to their attainment of primacy, because they avoid situations so structured or attempt to redefine such circumstances, they engage in actions which seem to be irresponsible.

College and high-school students are keenly aware in a negative way of this third conception of responsibility, and parents of children in slum schools also actively oppose it. If a teacher insists that students submit to his judgment or his authority, if his understandings and values are bases for indoctrination, that teacher tends to hold the students answerable for the assimilation and adoption of his position. He expects the students to be accountable without having allowed them the primacy of their needs. Similarly, if the subject matter that the students must learn is distant from their interests, their impulses, and their ready comprehension, the instructor is hard put to hold the students answerable for the learning of the subject matter without committing himself to a separation of accountability from primacy. When students complain that college or high school is not relevant to them, they are saying that the subject matter is sufficiently far from their active lives that it fails to be of service to them; they are asserting that they resent being held accountable when they are not treated as primary agents.

What have these three definitions of responsibility to do with hierarchical arrangements in human relationships? The conception of responsibility that unites primacy and accountability is a central organizing factor in hierarchical systems of an equalitarian bent, as I have already asserted; the two conceptions that arise from the separation of primacy and answerability are now to be seen as major organizing principles in hierarchical systems of an authoritarian nature. In equalitarian systems each person is held accountable to all others in the system precisely to the degree that she is given or asserts primacy as innovator, person with veto power, decision-maker, etc. Conversely, within equalitarian systems when a person is held to account by members of the system, she is allocated primacy adequate

Commensalist expectations

to her answerability. The person is given as much authority as she must answer for.

In an authoritarian hierarchical arrangement two displacements take place from the splitting apart of the fundamental elements of responsibility. To put the matter simply, the person who is superior in the hierarchy may be granted or may take unto himself an excess of primacy; the person who is in the lower ranks may find himself excessively answerable. In the authoritarian manifestations of hierarchy the two aspects of responsibility press in opposite directions; accountability is directed upward more than downward so that each person is asked to be in some degree excessively subordinate to the person above, and primacy shrinks as one goes down the hierarchy so that each person is presumed to be more excessively the cause of events in an organization than the person below. The effects of these displacements accumulate so that the person at the top seems to have great primacy and the person at the bottom great answerability. The individual who is adapted to authoritarian hierarchy, the "authoritarian personality." is submissive to his superiors, often abjectly submissive, and he is domineering, frequently arrogantly domineering, to his inferiors.

We can take the whole society as illustrative of this point. Much has been written about the power of leaders of society, the so-called "ruling class," to dominate and control "the masses." The top, or "ruling class," in such a society, in accordance with its exaggerated primacy, would seem to have autonomy of interests, initiative, power to impress interests and initiative upon others, and freedom and rationality in the pursuit of its interests. The bottom, the oppressed, the "masses," would appear, according to the exaggerated answerability connected with their lot, dependent, manipulated, powerless, determined by others and irrational in the pursuit of their interests.

However, primacy and accountability cannot *in fact* be segregated successfully in concrete social relations. When a person, group, or class tries to be primary without being answerable, or accountable without being primary, when it *intends* this segregation, it calls forth counteractions that equalize, that tie together in practice all those involved. If a person tries to be primary without being accountable, then precisely to the degree that he is allotted primacy, he finds that others become mobilized to contest for primacy, to avoid the encounter, or to force accountability upon him. The ways in which this equalizing process takes place may vary according to whether the person is high or low in the hierarchy and according to the nature of the situation and the personality configurations of the participants. *But there will be an inevitable and persistent tendency to bind primacy and accountability together.* Human relations are always relations of equals; basic to that equality is the unity of primacy and accountability within responsibility. Persons may *intend* or strive for superior-inferior relations, but experience shows over and over again that they always *create* relations of equals.[2] Later in this essay I will be showing some of the ways in which this equalizing process proceeds.

Within this understanding that equality suffuses all human practice, the "ruling class" thus demonstrates a dichotomy between its appearance and its actual existence.

Appearance	*Actuality*
1) autonomy of interests;	1) pseudo-autonomy; dominated and compelled socially by a struggle for primacy without accountability;
2) initiative;	2) driven to discover and exploit initiatives lodged elsewhere; dependent upon initiative of others;
3) power to impress interests and initiative upon others;	3) possessed only of power allocated to it by all; power resides in the maintenance of faulty principles of organization by all in concrete social relations;
4) freedom and rationality in pursuit of its interests.	4) forced to pretend its primacy to avoid accountability; irrational when faulty principle of organization is activated as such, as object of focus.

The reverse situation holds for the "masses." Although they appear to be dependent victims of the control of others, they steadily re-create the system by their attempts to segregate primacy and accountability. They are active creators of the system as well as victims of its faults, to the same degree as the "ruling class." They are manipulative as well as manipulated, powerful as well as powerless, self-determining as well as determined by others.

I think this analysis suggests both positive and negative rhetorical properties connected with depictions of the "ruling class" as the prime enemy of the "masses." On the plus side, when we associate the whole principle of primacy without accountability with the "ruling class," we can divorce ourselves from complicity in sustaining that faulty principle of organization, and we can by this means come to an objective understanding of it. We make a part (the "ruling class") stand for the whole (all of society's members) so that we can examine that part intensively. The "ruling class" is seen as the sole beneficiary of it, and as singularly devoid of any of the problems deriving from its inadequacies. This fiction enables us to formulate how destructive the faulty principle is for most of us, that is, the "masses," and since most of us are part of the "masses" rather than of the "ruling class," we begin to realize the weaknesses within our society.

This seems to be the meaning of Kenneth Burke's "Ultimate Stage" in the following quote.

"'Hierarchy' is the old, eulogistic word for 'bureaucracy,' with each stage employing a rhetoric of obeisance to the stage above it, and a rhetoric of charitable condescension to the stage beneath it, in sum, a rhetoric of courtship, while all the stages are infused with the spirit of the Ultimate Stage, which sums of the essence implicit in the hierarchic mode of thought itself, and can thus be 'ideologically' interpreted as its 'cause.'"[3]

On the negative side, however, stands the necessary concomitant of distortion, the penalty for victimizing the "ruling class" by making it assume in our minds the entire burden of the faulty principle of organization that is in fact maintained by all, including the "masses." We fail to diagnose just this role of the "masses" in the perpetual recreation of society according to the rules underlying this principle of organization. All are oppressed by all; there are no special villains. We are our own enemies. Some of us are more our own enemies only in that we are more dedicated at a given moment to the continuation of the faulty principle of organization, and we are enemies only to the degree and during the period that we defend this principle.

Those persons trying to change authoritarian systems into equalitarian ones, basing their organizing efforts on a political line that attributes all power and most evil to the "ruling class," must fail in their purpose if my understanding is correct. When they overestimate the power of the "ruling class," when they glorify the freedom, self-aggrandizement, personal gain of those on top, they imply that the answer to problems in society lies in overcoming the current leadership, in exacting more answerability at the top. But to be rid of the "ruling class" is never to be rid of the few persons who occupy positions at the top of the hierarchy; the "ruling class" disappears when the society is free from the principle of organization which attempts to segregate primacy and accountability in concrete social relations. That which is true for society in general is also true for all its sub-systems, all its institutions and all its people. It is never sufficient merely to oust those at the top. Usually, the group replacing them repeats their errors. All participants must be part of an effort to reform their methods of interpreting and allocating responsibility.

III

An authoritarian system produces problems for everyone in it because by its very nature it pits primacy and accountability against each other rather than fostering their mutual and integrated expression. The nature of the problem varies. Thus, for a person of an equalitarian bent, who balances primacy and accountability when she tries to be responsible, a distinct series of problems is raised by the authoritarian organization. Her efforts violate both the primacy and answerability dictates of the institution. For a person who acts from an authoritarian view of responsibility, either overstressing primacy or exaggerating accountability, problems take a different form. When she emphasizes primacy, she is faced with problems in answerability; when she emphasizes answerability, she is made to deal with her failures of initiative.

Generally speaking, as long as a person's moves toward equalitarianism are of minor influence or imperfectly perceived by those who defend the system, the person is left free to practice his equalitarianism. The caseworker can quietly permit primacy to his client so that the client becomes reassured and in response tends to become answerable to the requirements of the institution. The teacher can diminish student accountability, as by lowering the intrusion of grades and examinations upon the educational process, and can elevate student primacy so that personal equality is developed. The police officer who is respectful to the kids on the street, who keeps an eye out for them without threatening them or hounding them develops real bonds with them.

Some equalitarian behavior is acceptable in autocratic circles, therefore, but it is acceptable only when it is limited, exceptional and not too noticeable. When a person's equalitarian actions go beyond these narrow limits, he finds himself in one or another of four focal conflicts of interest produced by the tendency of the system to maintain and protect itself. Usually variants of all four conflicts become active when equalitarianism intrudes upon authoritarianism, but the emphasis is one time upon one focal conflict and another time upon a different one.

1. **An individual may redistribute to persons lower in the hierarchy the excessive share of primacy allocated to the superior by the authoritarian hierarchical arrangement; the implicit purpose is to correct the displacement of primacy toward the higher positions in the hierarchy.**

By this correction, the balance between the two elements of responsibility is promoted. A correction of this sort is a standard of professional social caseworkers, for example, and has led to the continuing demand for greater freedom of movement in service activities by those low in the administrative hierarchy but highly trained in a profession. Vinter, in "The Social Structure of Service," speaks directly to this issue:

"Professionals take considerable pride in their technical skills and prefer initiative and self-direction in the use of these skills. Limits are placed on practitioner initiative and autonomy through supervision, however able the supervisor may be in exercising her authority. This analysis suggests that claims to autonomy are greater among fully trained and experienced practitioners. Under such circumstances it is expected that strain between professional and administrative orientations increases....

"Strain also arises from the juxtaposition of the nonauthoritarian ideology of social work and the exercise of authority and control within the administrative context. Valuation of autonomy and self-determination for the client has pervaded the administrative structures of social welfare, reinforcing distinctively professional claims to independence."[4]

These ideas of initiative, self-direction, autonomy, professional independence, and self-determination for the client all refer to the subject of primacy as the cause of events in which an actor is engaged. Elsewhere in his article Vinter refers to a "significant downward shift of decision-making powers" that "reduces the effective authority of the supervisor...." Again, with decision-making powers and effective authority he touches upon the primacy issue.

2. **An individual may attempt to diminish accountability from below to above in the hierarchy so that the excessive share of answerability is sloughed off.**

The implicit purpose is to promote the balance of the two components of responsibility by lessening the weight of accountability in lower positions until it becomes proportionate to the primacy allocated to the higher positions in the authoritarian hierarchical arrangement. This weakening of answerability at one level is the reverse side of the strengthening of primacy. The insistence upon greater initiative, autonomy, self-direction, decision-making power may mean the demand for greater primacy in the hands of the recipient of initiative, or it may mean less dependence upon a superior for a detailed reckoning of the subordinate's actions and decisions.

In a report on "Educational Innovation" at Princeton University during the 1960s, Simon describes an attempt to downgrade answerability from students to professors:

"The reformers are disturbed that the traditional methods encourage the student to memorize more than to create, to repeat more than to think, to answer more than to question. They deplore the passive nature of so much of college education, and they have begun to ask how much filling requirements, doing assignments and taking tests promote knowledge and understanding which is personally meaningful. Their goal is to develop an education which promotes deep and creative thinking by restoring initiative and responsibility to the student. To this end, the experiments free the students in various ways of some of the formal restraints and encourage them to concentrate on intensive, critical, independent study. Test have been abolished or de-emphasized, and papers and reports are stressed ... specific assignments have been replaced by long bibliographies from which students choose to read what interest them."[5]

The large-scale systematic attempts to lessen accountability (which increases primacy at the same time, as seen in the quote above) pertains mainly to lower levels in hierarchies and can be seen in the rise of professionalism and unionism in public service fields like social welfare, education, law enforcement, nursing and mental health care in large state hospitals. The professional social worker holds himself accountable to professional values as well as to the agency in which he works; he is thereby enabled to be less subservient to administrators in the agency. In higher education, similarly, professors commonly refuse to allow any supervision in academic matters by other than faculty members ("We are not employees of the university"), thus downgrading answerability to administrators, trustees, and the community, while maintaining accountability to their peers and their students.

In more authoritarian settings, like public assistance agencies and the less known colleges and universities, this reliance upon professionalism is neither encouraged nor permitted. Professionally trained caseworkers have a hard time in established public welfare settings precisely to the degree they assume they can be less answerable and take more initiative; professors in the autocratically run colleges who possess outstanding competence face the same problem. In these authoritarian organizations we increasingly find the turn toward unionizing so that in the adversarial confrontation between union and management (administration) the accountability of caseworkers and professors inside the institution is lowered. Because they do not have significant decision-making power, people lower in the hierarchy protect themselves against the disproportionate answerability expected of them.

3. **An individual may attempt to increase the accountability from above to below so that the excess primacy in the higher positions is balanced by an additional answerability.**

In the heyday of civil rights activism, a major effort of the social movement in black communities within major American cities was directed toward decentralization of the large bureaucratic public service institutions. The demand was made that police departments be decentralized and policemen and women become responsible to the needs of the community. Some groups insisted that each community have the power to discipline the police officers who worked in their neighborhood. Similarly, in large cities the move toward decentralizing school boards was directed toward increasing the answerability of persons within the school system to members of the community they served.

The problem that surfaced — when police officers and teachers were held to account by the consumers of their service (by their "subordinates" in the hierarchy) — was that injustices perpetrated by authoritarian systems were transferred rather than alleviated. Police officers and teachers, not police chiefs and superintendents, absorbed this accountability — and because police officers and teachers are low in the hierarchies of their respective institutions, they already suffered from excessive accountability. A significant part of the improper treatment of citizens by police officers was found to stem directly from the authoritarian administration of police forces in which the patrolmen were (and continue to be) assigned tasks far beyond their training, their capacity to understand, and their actual authority, and they were then held strictly accountable by the courts and other authorities in the legal world. Among other failings, they were not given assistance in dealing with their personal fears and uncertainties since it was assumed they were emotionally sturdy and were not to reveal dependency.

In a like way social caseworkers in public welfare agencies are degraded by being given tough assignments with inadequate attention to their personal needs and requirements in the implementation of these assignments. It is frightening and depressing to have continuous contact with oppression and oppressed people. Unless the fears, dismay, and hopelessness of the caseworkers are aired among workers within the welfare organization through such means as case conferences, personal supervision, general sharing of experiences between workers, and other communal arrangements, these very understanable emotional reactions to the clients and their situation become transformed into antagonism toward the clients. Social caseworkers resent the clients for making them unhappy and for frustrating their attempts to be helpers, and the caseworkers are not alone in this reaction. School teachers show the same symptoms, as do policewomen and men and nurses.

The community failed in its purpose of pushing toward decentralization when it did not at the same time force or create within the institutions a rectification of the displacements of primacy and accountability. For success, police lieutenants and principals must be made more accountable to police officers and teachers, as well as everyone in the institution being made answerable to the community; and judges must be made to answer to police officers at the same time police are asked to account for their actions. The entire organizational pattern within the hierarchy needs to undergo revision, and in the reformation citizens and patrolmen and women, students and teachers, patients and nurses become partners rather than antagonists.

4. **An individual may attempt to diminish excess primacy from higher to lower levels in the hierarchy.**

The implicit purpose of such an effort is to balance the two components of responsibility by lowering the primacy of superiors. The lowering of primacy makes it proportionate to their answerability to subordinates. Because this attempt constitutes a direct attack upon the "authority' or "power" of the leadership, it is the most explosive form of intrusion made by equalitarianism upon an authoritarian hierarchical system. It is easier for persons lower in a hierarchy to call for greater answerability from above or for a greater role in decision-making than it is to call for an outright, direct diminution of the primacy allocated to the leader.

There is good reason why a challenge to the excess primacy of leaders is the most provocative of all equalitarian encroachments. The authoritarian hierarchical system in industrial societies is erected upon the idea that the person with initiative, the innovator, the risk-taker, is properly elevated to leadership in organizations. The very organizing principle that makes hierarchies authoritarian derives most clearly from the permission to operate given to persons who take unto themselves more primacy than they are accoutable for. The assault upon the excess primacy of the leaders, the most obvious challenge to authoritarianism, is almost the only one of the four focal conflicts produced by an equalitarian set of actions that is recognized for what it is. Power to the leader is the mark of authoritarianism understood by everybody, and confrontation that attacks this power alignment is likely to be fraught with intensity of attack and defense.

Persons who live by an equalitarian form of the distribution of responsibility have a sense of the nature of good human relations, and they are consequently among the best caseworkers, police officers, teachers and nurses. They have competence, they perform their work adequately and they bring about a positive response to their endeavors from those whom they are serving. Kids on the street know to identify the decent police officers — they have a great need to know — and they show great respect for these police men and women. So too, fair professors are honored and good caseworkers revered.

The smoothness that characterizes encounters between teachers and students in such cases, however, is not always paralleled by equal honor and respect for the teacher by her colleagues and superiors. In an organization structured in such a way as to promote inequality, ambivalence frequently arises toward the teacher who is equitable. That person is admired for her performance and her willingness to defy the authoritarian system, she is resented for her success and her unwillingness to defer to superiors or to the requirements of the institution. Colleagues and administrative superiors look at the able teacher or police officer from their own perspective and see her not as unifying primacy and accountability, but as herself aiming to be primary while rejecting full accountability in the organization. In a real sense, they are correct in their judgment. When a person behaves in an equalitarian manner within an authoritarian system, she is regulating herself by something beyond the requirements established by persons at the upper levels of the hierarchy and beyond the demands of the system itself. Were she adapted to the authoritarian hierarchical system, she would behave in an authoritarian way, she would accept answerability upward and primacy downward. But her authoritarianism is proof of an unwillingness to accept this arrangement and she can be seen to have taken unto herself greater primacy in the determination of events than is allotted to her and, implicitly, lesser answerability.

Apart from coming to terms with requirements for conformity within the authoritarianism in the institution, the individual of equalitarian temperament or intention must handle a bitter irony. Because the police officer, nurse, aide, or caseworker who adheres to an equalitarian style is productive in his work, he often promotes the acceptance of the police force, clinic, mental hospital or public welfare agency as *it is*. The man who defies or ignores the norms of the status quo finds himself a significant force in the continued maintenance of those very norms. Without the able work of the equalitarian members of the staff, each of these organizations would have fewer redeeming qualities and opposition would have an easier road to follow. The organizations are not all bad — they have good services rendered by these few members — and the organizations therefore are taken to be reasonably acceptable.

One further element defeats or demoralizes the equalitarian person in an autocratic institution: she may be promoted into the higher levels of the institution. As a consequence of her new position, the individual finds that she has greater primacy as a causative or initiating agent, but limitations are placed upon her being accountable to those at the lower levels. Because subordinates are likely to be deferent to her as they accommodate to the norms of the organization, and as they use their past experience, they do not accept easily the increased answerability that the superior attempts to register. Also, when the individual is promoted into the higher ranks, she tends to lose contact with the clients who are receiving the services of the organization. The good teacher becomes a department chair or principal and has different relations to the students. The good caseworker becomes a superior or agency administrator. With the decline in her direct dealing with clients, the pattern of rewards and satisfactions for the worker begins to change. She becomes more reliant upon institutional goals for personal satisfactions and she gradually slips into the norms of the organization. This has been a common outcome of the successes of affirmative action for women and minorities.

IV

If equalitarian behaviors in an authoritarian system are not trouble free, they are still preferable to authoritarian behaviors. On the one hand, with all the difficulties they arouse, equalitarian actions tend to be more invigorating and rewarding than actions based on authoritarianism. On the other hand, trouble within the authoritarian system does not come always from equalitarian strivings; it also rises from actions determined by fixed personality styles that mimic the organizing principles of the hierarchy. Some people have as a personality trait the tendency to construct their behaviors as if to assume primacy without being accountable; others attempt to be answerable beyond their position of primary agent. Special difficulties can be traced to the operations of these personality traits within authoritarian hierarchical arrangements.

1. **An individual occupying a lower position in an hierarchy may repeatedly attempt to assert vis-a-vis someone in a higher position greater primacy in events than is permitted by the system and lesser answerability than that which is required by the system.**

The person behaves in such a way as to express the personality trait that takes primacy as the sole component of responsibility. He works from the assumption that he will always be exploited, cheated or harmed (i.e., the authoritarian assumption), and the only counteraction to such an outcome is for him to be responsible for the encounter. Repeated attempts of this sort are typical of clients in public welfare agencies, as I have already suggested, and their transactions with caseworkers reveal remarkable exemplifications of futility in putting forth the same interest over and over in a situation that is organized in opposition to that interest.

The clients spin many variations on the theme of primacy-without-accountability as the client-caseworker encounters go round and round without significant engagement or development. On the one hand, the clients act to impose their primacy; the caseworkers respond by demanding answerability or by asserting their own primacy. Hostile, competitive struggles inevitably ensue. On the other hand, the clients do not allow transactions to unfold into completion unless they are primary agents in the transactions. Because primacy is seen as the last or only area in which the clients can maintain their autonomy and integrity, they become masters of the art of postponement, of promising to carry out an obligation at a later time, of avoiding encounters in which it has already been established that they will not achieve primacy. Herein lies the source of their apparent irresponsibility. They cannot and will not abide by the primacy of others and they make promises under duress when others are in charge. Because their promises were forced from them, they feel justified in not carrying out the obligations they have seemingly taken on.

2. **An individual occupying a spot in a hierarchy other than the lowest level may maximize the excess primacy at that level and avoid the issue of accountability.**

Her implicit purpose is to implement a personality trait that takes primacy as the sole component of responsibility. The personality trait of the individual and the character of the social structure are in certain respects in mutual adjustment in that the person needs primacy and the social system allocates it to her. Persons who are driven by personality needs to make the most of the excess primacy available in authoritarian hierarchical systems are among the most "successful" bureaucrats and entrepreneurs. They make a career of innovating, initiating, inaugurating, starting new enterprises. For the implementation of what they have put in motion, these persons rely upon other members of the organizations to which they belong; they consider themselves to have done their job when the start has been made. They do take credit, however, for the accomplishments that follow from their initiative, and on the basis of such credit, they tend to rise in bureaucracies.

In order to be in a position to initiate new trends, these people are constantly on the alert for the newest happenings in significant places. They are keenly sensitive to all the beginning fads and fashions, scouting distant places to detect the rising idea, procedure, way of doing something, and bringing these home to the organization for introduction as an innovation. They are the risk-takers who do not absorb the penalties when the risk fails; they are the decisive decision-makers who pass accountability downward when their choices are found to be faulty. Consequently, they do better by moving from position to position rather than by remaining in one place over an extended period of time. They can succeed by rapid promotion or by switching from one organization to another, or, most perfect for this type of individual, by rapid promotion while going from one organization to another. The type is familiar. *We fail only to recognize the fact that such persons are compelled to initiate, and unless checked by outside forces, will push on into personal and organizational disaster.*

If the personality trait of the individual and the norm of the authoritarian hierarchical system are adjusted to each other, that is, if the person driven to initiate operates in a system that permits excessive primacy, he also brings into play excessive answerability that then must be absorbed by those in inferior positions in the hierarchy. The subordinates must do the work initiated by the superior, and they must take the blame if it comes. They must acknowledge that credit for their efforts is to be given to the superior. Consequently, they tend to undermine this systematic diminishing of their contributions in any way that is open to them, by sabotaging the quality of the work, by avoiding blame, or by gathering credit to themselves.

A person who maximizes excess primacy at any level in a hierarchy offends not only those in inferior positions; he also threatens those in superior positions. His personality trait is based on attention to primacy and neglect of answerability, but his alignment as subordinate to a superior calls for him to defer to the judgments of that superior. The very characteristic of his personality that makes him adjusted to the system when he is in a superior slot makes him maladjusted when he is in the inferior place.

Superiors, sensing a threat to their primacy, demand accountability from this kind of subordinate as soon as they become aware of his tendency to maximize excess primacy; at that point it becomes his turn to temporize. Like the client in welfare, he becomes an artist in postponement, displacement, avoidance of completion in encounters. Unlike the client, he can often shunt to lower levels the accountability that is thrust upon him. Indeed, his success in having subordinates take on his accountability to the satisfaction of his superiors is the key to further promotion for the entrepreneur.

The client in public welfare, like certain of these successful bureaucrats and self-made millionaires, believes that responsibility means only initiative; these types of persons are similar to each other also in that they sooner or later find themselves in reverberating cycles in which struggles with others take on the constraints of repeated and vain attempts to resolve problems caused by their fixed ways of acting. At some point they run away or are catapulted out from the system in which they have become entrapped. It happens sooner with clients, late with entrepreneurs, but it happens in the long run to each person compelled to live out a personality trait that violates the intrinsic trend toward equality that controls human relations.

3. **An individual occupying a higher position in a hierarchy may repeatedly attempt to offer someone in a lower position greater answerability than is permitted by the norms of the system and lesser primacy than what is required by the system.**

Her implicit purpose is to give vent to a personality trait that takes accountability as the sole component of responsibility. Women, trained to attend to relationships and connections, may be more likely to manifest this personality trend. Because the personality trait of the individual and the character of the social structure are distinctly at odds with each other, trouble for the individual is a natural outcome. A good instance of this particular form of responsibility is contained in a review by Frank Jellinek of John Womack Jr.'s *Zapata and the Mexican Revolution:*

> "Zapata himself was at a subjective disadventage here. He had an almost neurotic, if wholly justified, distrust of politicians....
>
> "Mr. Womack has hit off Zapata's character in a way which has never been bettered; 'in some uncanny way the common people of Morelos had picked a leader they could not be surer of, that is, Zapata could not have felt more responsible towards them. A man obsessed with staying true, he could not betray a promise for the life of him. But courage of one kind can hint at cowardice of another, and Zapata was afraid [of a vital meeting with some politicians] — not for himself, but of himself, of unwittingly betraying the trust his peers and their people had invested in him.'"[6]

This illustration is excellent in its description of a personality trait (witness the use of the concept of "character" and the adjectives of "neurotic" and "obsessed") and, in particular, the trait built around responsibility-as-answerability-only. It also adds a vital element, namely, the appearance of the trait in a leader, one high in a hierarchy. The counterpart of this trait, primacy-as-responsibility, was found to be strongly self-defeating when found in the lower echelons of a hierarchy precisely because in authoritarian systems the displacement of primacy is upward; similarly, Zapata, from his high post, violated a system of downward displacement of accountability by his need to answer to his followers, and, if Mr. Womack is right, this preoccupation was very costly to him. A revolutionary must be strongly oriented toward accountability to his followers, but this orientation must not overshadow his willingness to assert initiative on their behalf.

4. **An individual occupying a place in a hierarchy other than the highest level may maximize the excess answerability at that level**

and avoid the issue of primacy.

His implicit purpose is to implement in action a personality trait that takes accountability as the sole component of responsibility. The personality trait of the individual and the character of the social structure are in certain respects in mutual adjustment; the person very much needs to be accountable, the social system fosters excessive answerability in an upward-looking direction.

Persons who are compelled to live out this personality trait are among the most reviled individuals in any system. They are held in contempt not only by their peers and subordinates but also by those to whom they report. The hallmark of this trait is the adoption of a slavish role to a superior through whom one achieves her own purposes. To be excessively accountable in its mildest form is to be uncritically loyal, selflessly devoted, a strict adherent to the formal rules and conventions and the informal guidance of the superior. Those who maximize the answerability from lower to higher levels, who are the extremists for this personality trait, are known by many names: sycophants, Uncle Toms, informers, yes men, company spies, finks, flatterers and so forth. They are the counterparts to the wild risk-takers and are to be found in equal measure in organizations that harbor the extremes of primacy displaced upward, accountability downward.

If the person at the top of a hierarchy is driven by a strong urge to be primary cause of all events in which he participates, very close to that person will be found his flatterer, his yes man. Gradually throughout the system grow pairs of such individuals, the innovator and the loyalist, the decision-maker and the individual skilled at calming the disturbances produced by his actions.

V

I have outlined a number of problems that are common to authoritarian hierarchical systems. Whether one works from a equalitarian disposition or an authoritarian one, living and working in an authoritarian system cannot be accomplished without significant costs. There is no satisfactory way to live within an authoritarian hierarchy. The only human solution involves the transformation of authoritarian hierarchies into equalitarian hierarchies, and this must be done at every level of the hierarchy since the very organizing principles of hierarchy are at stake. It is not adequate to change part of the system, say at the lower levels such as may be exemplified by caseworker-client relations, because over time that part of the system will be made to conform to the norms of the total. Similarly, it will not do merely to change the relations between extremes. It is fantasy to think that the workers must become the managers, the patients, the doctors, the students become the faculty or trustees, without also insisting upon major alterations in every superordinate-subordinate human relationship within the hierarchical system. No change short of reformation of the entire systematic bias that affects all members of an organization will be adequate.

In the next chapter I have suggestions to make about such efforts to remake systems when one is a subordinate in them.

Notes

1. Ms. Jeanne C. Pollock and I collaborated in this work in which we were assisted by Dr. L. Diane Bernard, the late Ms. Miriam Krentzlin and Dr. Edmund Sherman. We have published the outcome of our studies and the present essay is an extension of the thinking of these published articles. The publications are: "Responsibility as a Personality Characteristic." *A.M.A. Archives of General Psychiatry,* 1967, Volume 17; and "Clients and the Sense of Responsibility." *Public Welfare,* 1967, Volume 25.

2. Cf. John Macmurray. *The Clue to History.* New York: Harper, 1939.

3. Kenneth Burke. *The Rhetoric of Motives.* New York: Prentice-Hall, 1950.

4. Robert D. Vinter. "The Social Structure of Service." In: *Behavior Science for Social Workers,* Edwin J. Thomas, Editor. New York: Free Press, 1967.

5. William H. Simon. "Educational Innovation." *Princeton Alumni Weekly,* 1968, Volume 69.

6. Frank Jellinek. Review of *Zapata and the Mexican Revolution* by John Womack Jr. *New York Times Book Review,* February 2, 1969.

CHAPTER 7

TOWARD EQUALITY: UP AND AGAINST

I

Most of the institutions in which we live and work these days are more or less authoritarian. Not only industry and commercial enterprises, but government, health and welfare institutions, educational centers and other institutions generally assumed to be democratic are run according to hierarchies that are autocratic in function. When we are subordinates subjected to unjust authority, we become aware of the way in which our very integrity is undermined. From our sense of helplessness and anger, we act impulsively and defensively. Most of us find ourselves as subordinates in authoritarian settings, not just a few times, but often and repeatedly, and this whether we are high or low in position in the hierarchies. Along the way to total reformation of these organizations, and as a part of the effort, we need to develop ways for conducting ourselves more successfully in these circumstances. In my view this involves acting to transform the authoritarian system into a more equalitarian one while at the same time achieving the goals of the organization and preserving one's place in it to the extent possible. I have some suggestions for pursuing this course.

II

Not too long ago, in a class in which I was explaining some of the ideas I will put forward in this essay, a woman phrased a thought that innocently promoted a misjudgment common in contemporary thought, one that is influential in professional education and professional practice as well as in daily life in organizations. We had been talking about how important to a therapeutic relationship between a clinical social worker and client is the equalitarian attitude fostered by the social worker. The development of equality between people, I had been suggesting, is a central piece of any truly therapeutic action, and a worker cannot pay too much attention to this matter.

The student commented:
"I can see how a clinical social worker working with a client can introduce greater equality into the relationship, but I cannot imagine how one can similarly influence a supervisor, can introduce greater equality into a relation with an autocratic supervisor."

GETTING EVEN

On the surface of this thought is the idea that if one is interested in constructing personal relations of an equalitarian sort, it is easier to be a superior than to be and inferior. In other words, it appears to be simpler to share the power that is lodged in the superior position than to obtain equal influence when starting from an inferior or subordinate position.

A latent part of the student's thinking needs to be brought into focus so that we can readily perceive the limitations in its reasoning. The hidden assumption vital to her position is this: she had presumed that the relationship between the clinical social worker and the client is independent of the authoritarianism of the organization or, alternatively, that the relationship between them exists in a surrounding that fosters or permits the conduct of human affairs along equalitarian lines. The assumption she made is that the clinical social worker is free to propose any form of relationship acceptable to the client and to himself or herself as worker, and that the client is similarly free of organizational constraints. Now it is indeed a relatively easy task for a clinical social worker to promote equality when the organization within which the therapeutic activity takes place permits the therapist full freedom in this regard and provides all the required resources. In a facilitating environment, most clinical social workers can institute equalitarianism if and when they so desire. But in such a setting it is equally open for the client to engage and challenge on an equal footing with the social worker; what makes it possible for the clinical social worker to foster equality also establishes an environment in which it is possible for the client to take similar equalitarian initiatives.

In an authoritarian setting, though, the situation is changed. The clinical social worker is not free; she is constrained by the principles of organization which control the relationship so that actually it is not an easy task for her to introduce equality. It is precisely this fact that the young woman student had not taken into account. Therapist and client may have different functions, different positions, and different tasks, but they are commonly bound by the social situation in which they act. The reason many clinical social workers who sincerely hold equalitarian ideologies find themselves acting in a contrary way — at best paternally, at worst in a petty, tyrannical fashion — is most probably that they are caught in the web of the authoritarian settings in which they work.

Students in a professional school should be more keenly alert than most individuals to this dilemma, and they almost are, since they move back and forth between the roles of student and professional worker. In social work, for instance, the student is expected to be concurrently counselor to his client, apprentice to his supervisor, and learner with his classroom teacher. Because he is somewhat sheltered by his educators, he is able to practice more freely than regular employees of agencies; his protected condition often allows him to be the conscience of the agency, the goad to change, the challenge to the status quo, though there are limits to how much he can experiment with equalitarianism.

I have said that students are *almost* alert to the notion that superiors are constrained to the same degree as subordinates by the principles of organization of any institution. However, since the students are not as expert or accomplished as their supervisors and teachers, merely by reason of having less practical experience, they are vulnerable to self-doubt and uncertainty. They have been trained in obedience over the years, as have we all, and they have learned the lessons of submission too well. As subordinates, students are subjected to all the fears involved in facing autocratic superiors. They are led to exaggerate their own weakness and at the same time overemphasize the strength of the superior. They hesitate to confront and contend, and their reluctance in the sphere of action is reflected in their self-effacing opinions; or they overextend themselves in struggle and become disabled in the learning process by their own anger which takes on the form of rebellion.

Most students come to believe it is wiser to compromise in school so that, having achieved the professional degree without being labeled as troublemakers, they can then become persons of authority who will exert influence in agencies and the community, and who will then be able to promote greater freedom in their relationships with clients. The compromise is fatal. It is the very capitulation to the authoritarian nature of professional practice that inhibits the expression of equalitarianism in the development of effective service. The willingness to compromise in actions in school leads to the failure to articulate clearly limits surrounding the power of superiors.

The widespread misconception is that persons higher in a hierarchy are freer from the imperatives of the organizational principles of institutions than are persons occupying lower slots in the hierarchical formation. The opinion held by students is representative of the general belief that the higher the position a person holds, the more she can shape the organization according to personal preference and the more she is independent of the contextual social and historical forces that are connected with that organization. In practice, however, the superior like the subordinate is dominated by the modes of relation which are characteristic of the social institution, that is, which are created and recreated routinely by all who participate in the life of that institution. One's personal style is allowed influence only insofar as it does not challenge the organization's boundaries.

A subordinate seeking equality soon becomes aware of some of the built-in barriers to this aim in authoritarian settings, particularly those that have already limited him or her directly. The barriers that such a person usually overlooks, however, are those that also hamper the superior. In another situation when the same person assumes the role of a superior, he or she becomes keenly aware of the ready limitations upon his or her autonomy. The sense of powerlessness that pervades our social existences, thus, stems from our experiences both as superiors and as subordinates, but we tend to associate that sense with our underside activities alone.

Unfortunately, professional social work education too often institutionalizes this perspective, thereby fostering resignation in the face of profound problems. In professional schools we teach students more how to be an authority in regard to clients than how to transform autocratic relations into equalitarian ones by working from many positions in hierarchies. Emphasis is placed upon how to diagnose and treat clients, how to create practical community organizations, etc., rather than upon how to diagnose and treat faulty systems by acting in concert with many forces within and without that system. Overstressing the powers of the professional as an authority, we promise greater results from that distortion than we can ever produce. The consequence is that our students learn to fake their competence or else lower their goals

III

When we find ourselves in the midst of autocratic domination as subordinates, we often are tempted to avoid direct struggle in the hope of diminishing the threat. Because we expect that it will lead either to a increase of oppression or ultimately to our ejection from the organization, we renounce open, immediate counteraction. Examples from past experience that seem to confirm such an expectation are readily available, since we all know people who have been outspoken and have paid for their audacity through being fired, expelled, excommunicated, imprisoned, or otherwise punished.[1]

Although it may appear that we are spared the danger of reprisal, we fail to achieve our true purpose when we deny to ourselves the risk and the challenge of dealing with the autocracy that oppresses us in the present. Accommodation to oppression may apparently succeed, in that we are not immediately cast out from the institution, and some among us, or even many, may rise to higher levels within the hierarchy. Nevertheless, such accommodation, rather than diminishing oppression, encourages and further promotes it. Self-denial by subordinates fails to impress autocrats; instead it urges them on. The resentment, anger, and related feelings that must be renounced, these pieces of the subordinate's life that are part and parcel of her actions in the organization, do not disappear; they are displaced and released at times when the person cannot control them. The renunciation of one's personal integrity makes one a foreigner to herself. The self-hatred that accompanies resignation in the face of domination leads not only to increased passivity in social relations, but to passivity in dealing with oneself and one's inner life. We become victims of that which we put away from ourselves. And as our experiences start to happen to us rather than come forth from and fulfill us as persons, so then we begin to call forth regulation from the outside — we look to autocratic systems to help us put down the wilder, renounced parts of ourselves.

Thus we live in the presence of a range of oppressive situations. We cannot successfully put down our opposition to oppression, much as we may want to accommodate and avoid the difficulties and uncertainties that we foresee; consequently, we swing over to the conterpart of submission, rebellion. We attempt to maintain our opposition through rebellion by overturning the superior and becoming the dominant element in the relation or by at least obtaining a new, more benevolent superior. We harbor the expectation that because the autocratic actions of the incumbent superior are a function of his personality, a different person will behave in a completely new way. We like to imagine, for instance, that we would be equalitarian if we were the authority, whatever the constraints of the organization and its members. We believe that we would not take advantage of underlings were we given similar responsibility.

Rebellion which relies upon change of individuals within roles accepts the authoritarianism of the system. In the desire to replace the people occupying the superior roles, we ignore the fact that superiors as well as subordinates are influenced by the authoritarianism of the system. The alternative to renouncing the present, emptying the frightening immediate, is to seek all in the present through rebellion and to be impatient with the long run. We try to act now, change the institution quickly, by means of more favorable leadership, to break down all obstacles through sharp, selective, well-directed assaults.

But rebellion against oppression must fail as much as submission. Rebellion does not handle the problem that we all contribute to the authoritarianism of the system, that we must all change and be changed so that our every action is more fundamentally equalitarian than authoritarian. Rebellion underestimates the self-transformation of all members of an organization that must necessarily accompany any shift away from autocratic systems.

If submission and rebellion represent lines of approach to oppression that fail to alleviate the pressure of authoritarianism, indeed, which paradoxically maintain and increase autocratic behavior, yet they cannot be all wrong; too many people, too regularly, move toward these solutions for them to be simply inappropriate. There must be ingredients from both renunciation of the opposition and from insistent struggle that pertains to remaking authoritarian into equalitarian organizations. We would do well then to search out the positive elements in these tactics as well as their faults.

From rebellion derives the principle that it is necessary to contend directly with oppression; from submission comes the principle that it is necessary to survive within the system lest the counteraction lose all purpose and we be swallowed up through the struggle. Seen together, these principles tell us that transformation of a system depends upon the development of conditions and tactics which promote struggle and survival, survival and struggle, for all members of that system. Each individual in the system (and that will include superiors and subordinates) must both contend with oppression and be able to survive in order to persist in that effort. An example of this principle was cited by Che Guevara in his theory of guerrilla warfare and he was destroyed by his inattention to this principle later in his career: the band must oppose the forces of power in the society but must survive to continue the opposition. Without direct opposition, the band is no counterforce; without survival, the band is disillusionment to the masses, a contribution to resignation.[2]

In the reach of our lives, accordingly, there must be a constant state of tension between our line of opposition and our line of survival; we must always see ourselves on the edge between opposing too much or too little in our roles as subordinates, as well as encouraging too much or too little opposition in our roles as superiors. The penalty we each pay for avoiding this fragile balance is the experience of our own alternating submission and rebellion, vile hatred of ourselves and detestation of others when we are subordinates, and our experience of powerlessness and persecution when we are superiors.

GETTING EVEN

IV

One theme connected with the subversion of authoritarian systems, drawn from observations of successful therapeutic care of the mentally ill, is that each encounter between subordinates and superiors needs to be important in its own right. Unless the fullness of opposition and survival characterize each event, the distortions of alternating rebellion and submission are created and re-created by the participants in the interaction. The impetus for the development of therapeutic communities in hospitals stems from the knowledge that every event in the life of a patient impinges upon his basic expectations, and conditions his readiness to attend to particular instances with their unique potentials and subtleties. To say that every encounter must be taken as important is not to say that every one should consist primarily of oppostion between subordinate and superior; that would be rebellion pure and simple. If all occasions of coordinated effort degenerated into negation by one party of the efforts of the other, no foundations would exist for survival of the relationship.

All encounters in any system of ongoing relationships help to determine one's bias towards more or less domination in that system. When a subordinate attempts to diminish an encounter to avoid threats to her survival or to shield herself from the feats that necessarily go along with oppostition, she is merely encouraging oppression. Much authoritarianism persists simply because persons tire of making each moment vital and are overcome by the fatigue and despair that follow from repeatedly failing in that effort.

One clear lesson derived from the treatment of psychotic and other disturbed individuals is that a single interaction between therapist and patient often marks a critical turning point, a qualitative change in the patient's life. That moment usually involves the negation by the therapist of the customary patterns of behavior utilized by that patient; it is a time of opposition to the dominating-submitting tendencies of the patient. Just when and how such interactions will happen is quite unpredictable so that the therapist must be alert and make the most of every opportunity.

We do know that these events occur most frequently when patient and therapist are taking part in a continuing relationship. The singular moment is contained within a series of interactions, each of which has seemed relevant though not definitive, yet each of which has contributed to preparation for the big change. On the therapist's side, the various interactions provide a picture of the patient's ways of living, a comprehension of the special constellation of forces that guide the patient. The therapist, more often intuitively than logically, acquires an understanding of the patient that enables him to contradict the patient, to surprise him, or otherwise negate his manipulative tendencies while still keeping firm the bond that ties together patient and therapist in a common task. The intertwined efforts of opposition to the patient's unproductive demands and maintenance of the close relation to the patient constitute central ingredients of such therapeutic encounters. On the patient's side, the series of interactions lays the groundwork for trust in the therapist, a trust that the therapist will be independent of the patient's manipulations and yet not hurtful toward him. The patient comes to sense that he can be challenged while not dominated, differed with but nonetheless fulfilled. His authoritarian dispositions which are inherently self-destructive are transformed in an equalitarian transaction.

In every transaction in which autocratic elements intrude, therefore, there are contained immediate and long-term perspectives which need to be coordinated with each other. In the immediate, an event is important in the degree to which direct opposition to any domination takes place while continuation of the relation is assured. In the service of the long-run perspective, the interaction is used to build the base for the critical transaction that will be associated with change of the system as a whole. When the subordinate cannot oppose to the full degree the domination of his superior, he can still probe the essentials of the relation and make increasingly accurate diagnoses, with the aim of preparing for more successful oppositions-with-survival in the future.

In outline, the argument here presented goes as follows:

In moving authoritarian systems toward equalitarianism, each encounter is important.

To the degree that it is possible, autocratic behavior by a superior should be opposed directly by the subordinate. When the limit is reached at which opposition will become rebellion and survival demands submission, the subordinate must attend to active preparation of some kind for the long run if she is to have any hope of withstanding the oppression confronting her.

Obviously, long-term preparation is not a substitute for opposition in the immediate, nor is it the devitalization of the encounter, the emptying of the present for future gain. As opposition too easily reverts to rebellion, similarly, long-range preparation becomes submission when it is not finely balanced with a sense of the importance and usefulness of the present. Active preparation for the critical turning point entails keen analysis and feeling for the patterns that unfold over and over again, the regularities and rigidities that are behind domination and that are also its weakness. Intricate diagnosis is too often a tool for the superior in regard to the subordinate, too seldom a conscious weapon forged by the subordinate.

V

When I now try to develop some concrete ideas on how to maximize opposition while preserving survival in the immediacy of encounters with autocrats, I am beset with hesitations that stem from the desire to be taken seriously without my having been recognized in obvious, public combat that I have practiced these ideas and can assert that they are productive guides for action. But I overcome my doubts somewhat when I realize that the ideas on my mind are not all obvious, they have not all been said before, they come from real experiences, they have been validated by others who have been in struggle and have attended to them, and I continue to believe they may be useful. I see them less as suggestions to be followed directly, more as stimulants to the creative thought of those similarly engaged in efforts to create an equalitarian and democratic society. I believe we all underestimate the degree to which everyday life is a battle with authoritarianism. We have each developed our own means for fighting within these institutions and are daily building a body of expertise from our successes and failures. It is time that we begin to assert our insights and achievements more effectively, and begin to share them with others.

From my experience I have gradually become aware of three principles or guidelines that can help people maximize opposition while preserving survival in the immediacy of encounters with autocrats. These principles are intended to assist persons in directly opposing the autocratic behavior of a superior without becoming rebellious and without submitting. They will be useful primarily to those who aspire to be *agents* in contest with authoritarian systems. An agent is a person who acts with integrity and autonomy in choosing and deciding how he can best achieve his purposes. He represents himself authentically and he actively chooses how he behaves. In the present case, an agent also refers to the person who directs himself to pursuing equalitarianism as the underlying theme of organization for any institution in which he is engaged.

The three principles which I shall describe and illustrate are:
1. The agent in countering authoritarianism needs to **rely upon structural supports** to his position, supports upon which he considers and represents himself as dependent, though the agent decides his dependency for each occasion.
2. The agent in countering authoritarianism needs to **mobilize social supports** to his position, supports neither coerced from others nor relied upon by the agent beyond their direct manifestations.
3. The agent who opposes authoritarianism **circumvents, deflects or deflates struggles for personal superiority.**

1. The agent in countering authoritarianism needs to rely upon structural supports to his position, supports upon which he considers and represents himself as dependent, though the agent decides his dependency for the occasion.

The agent may have available structural supports of various kinds. For example, she may rely upon the inherent nature of the task that she is performing within the organization to which both she and the superior belong. Freud used to say — to patients who found the work of freely recounting all that entered their consciousness too demanding — that he understood their plight and would very much like to agree to their preference for not proceeding in that manner. But, he would continue, the task of psychoanalysis did not give him the freedom to relieve the patient of his discomfort in that way. It was necessary to their common goal that the patient should associate to ideas freely and it was therefore necessary for Freud to uphold the demands of the task.[3] Freud was relying upon the structural support contained by the nature of the task, a support which he ultimately defined but to which he was subjected as much as the patient.

Most tasks have an existence that is independent to some degree of the prescriptions put forth by the superior. The subordinate who would counter the authoritarianism of his superior, therefore, does well to know the work and its inherent requirements more thoroughly than anyone else. He should also come to know intimately the boundaries at which the task is defined from above and at which it is of itself, free in some way from outside definition and control. He then has reason to balance the demands from the superior with the inherent requisites of the task. What is gained by this act of weighing one against the other is the fundamental component necessary to an agent — choice.

The agent is not hypocritical in choosing to be dominated by the requirements of the work itself. Although it is tempting, she does not feign one attitude to the superior and also hold a separate, private analysis of what is really required. Were she to rely upon duplicity in her contest with the superior, she would be reliant upon personal cunning to obtain dominance rather than upon the true structural supports that exist to be tapped. She would find herself brought into the domain of rebellion, and would soon learn that in the effort she has distorted her own personality by segregating private and public convictions. The agent must consistently be genuine in her representations to the superior because she understands the nature of the task and believes that she is guided by that as well as by the commands of the superior. She may also approach the superior by assuming that person's genuine concern for the work until such time as this is demonstrated to be untrue.

There are serious limitations for the agent in depending upon task requirements as a counterforce to the false authority expressions of his superior. He cannot too frequently, too pointedly, or in too self-willed a fashion bring the matter into open encounters lest he give indications that this is a chosen tactic aimed more at imposing his will upon the superior than an effort directed to accomplishment of the task. The essence of this approach can be stated briefly: where the superior has gathered excessive, arbitrary, unshared authority in his relation to the subordinate, the latter, as agent, incorporates more of the reality of the task (the nature of the work is seen as a contributing authority in the labors of the subordinate) while refusing to engage in a dispute over personal superiority or personal difference. The agent should be genuinely responsive to both task and superior, attending closely to what is appropriate to the demands of each.

When subordinates utilize this approach successfully, they are often presented with a new challenge to their goal of equalitarianism. Superiors who wish to continue their personal domination without hindrance and who do not accept the positive value of successful performance tend to debase and degrade the work that has been used to diminish their personal power. They compel a redefinition of the task such that it is no longer of value to the counteracting agent. The attack upon the subordinate who expects to be treated in an equalitarian way is displaced to his "accomplice," the work itself. Since, more often than not, the power belongs to the superior to redefine the work, the subordinate is forced to accept the debasement in the short run in order that he may survive within the organization.

The subordinate may find that she must do work of a cheapened nature and shift her opposition to the long run. One way to continue opposition is to persevere in operating upon the highest form or level of the task that she can manage without invoking a renewal of the debasement. In the simplest case, the subordinate submits to the degradation at the time the superior proposes and enforces it and then returns to the more adequate conceptions of the task as soon as that is possible. If the subordinate accepts the lessened form of her task in the longer run, if she institutionalizes and makes more permanent the superior's degraded version of the work, then she casts aside her role of agent by becoming passive, and she gives up opposition to the autocracy. The person thus contributes to sustaining her own oppression. I think it can be stated quite fairly that the decline of craftmanship and pride in work in modern America represents persistent submission to autocratic control. What starts out as a force for domination from above and sabotage of the domination from below, ends up as investment in oppression by all concerned.

Another common development is for the subordinate to be promoted to higher levels in the organization, away from his direct area of mastery. To the degree that they are gifted in the work they do, teachers and engineers become administrators, research personnel become chiefs, machinists become foremen, professors become deans, psychiatric social workers become agency heads. Rather than raise the prestige and pay of these direct service activities, organizations promote gifted persons away from their given territory, thereby lessening the general capacity of subordinates to oppose autocratic endeavors. The ranks of the subordinates are systematically depleted of the persons who are most effective in combatting authoritarianism by means of their expert knowledge of the inherent nature of the work.

A second structural support upon which an agent may cast her reliance consists of the various rules, policies and laws of the institution to which subordinate and superior both belong. In American society, it is common for policies and laws to be considerably more democratic than the actual practices within the institutions, and in our struggles with personal domination, we too often overlook the possibilities inherent in these formal aspects of the organization. By this I do not mean "working within the system" as conservatives and liberals alike demand of all change agents precisely when they wish to neutralize these persons and their movements. Rather, I refer to creative adaptation of whatever equalitarian aspects of an organization already exist for the purpose of overcoming the authoritarian facets within it.

In the library of a small state college with which I was acquainted, an arbitrary and autocratic head librarian dominated her staff. She had established a "chain of command," insisting that all communication go up through that chain and down from her in the strictest way possible. Always, her position was used to aggrandize herself, inside the library and outside it as well. She considered that a suggestion or hint from her was the most powerful of orders to her staff, and a request from her staff or a proposal for action made by one of them was a usurpation of her authority. One day a pronouncement from the President of the school was issued to all faculty and staff of the college, including the library personnel. He announced that a major concern for the academic year was to be the furthering of more democratic human relations throughout the institution. The President's ruling, paternalistic as it was, was subsequently passed on by the head librarian as one which she was supporting. It was at this point that the librarian suddenly created contradictory positions for her relations with subordinates; to obey her previous and continued arbitrary demands would be to disobey the new requirement to act in a more democratic manner, and *vice versa*. Space was opened for staff to rely upon structural supports — the President's policy — in opposing the autocratic behavior of the librarian when it surfaced anew. Regardless of the lack of personal commitment to greater democracy on the part of the librarian, staff could themselves genuinely rely upon the policy requiring democratic human relations, though they must also have been prepared to weather objections by the librarian.

Similarly, in schools of social work students find themselves committed to separate institutions with distinct and often discrepant policies. The curriculum demands that these students prepare not only through classes in the university but also by working in agencies and organizations that are serving the social, welfare, health, educational and other needs of the society. The students are part of the school in regard to academic study and part of the agency when they do their "field work." Furthermore, the school establishes conditions that guide the training of students when they are in the agencies. When a student is active in his field work agency, therefore, he is subject to a double set of policies: those set by the agency for all its members and those created by the school for its students. There are numerous instances in which students are dominated by superiors in agencies; indeed, there is systematic domination stemming from the unconscious effort to socialize students into bureaucratic professionalism. The more equalitarian students learn to utilize their status as school members in countering this domination, relying upon those policies guiding education that foster greater practical participation in a democratic way in social welfare practices.

In these examples the structural support chosen by the agent is the more equalitarian rule or policy which exists alongside the authoritarian practices in the institution. A subordinate who is an agent in the efort to transform authoritarian into equalitarian systems recognizes her right to be dependent upon that which facilitates her purposes, a right held separately from favors or permission granted by a superior. Such an agent is working within the system in the sense of utilizing that part of the system that is aligned with her purposes; she is not working within the system in the sense of regulating her own behavior to accord with the primary governing principle that is authoritarian in nature. It is again important to stress that the agent is not hypocritical or manipulative, conspiratorial or destructive — as she is often made to feel and to act by an oppressive superior — but is merely making a straightforward choice of preferred options among all that are available. The original motive for selection of a policy upon which to place her dependency may have been the wish to oppose autocratic behavior, a motive that is worthy in its own right, but the more complex and considered motivation which guides her actual behavior includes appropriate allegiance to preferred rules and policies.

In addition to the structural supports available from the nature of the job and the rules and policies in any organization are the alternate demands upon the agent that are connected with other groups of which he is a member. Most immediately relevant are such groups as labor unions and professional associations which have been recognized more or less by the offending institution. Less frequently useful, but not to be overlooked, are other groups such as family, church, one's family physician or local conventional opinions and pressures.

The same principles that have been outlined above apply here. The agent casts his dependency, simply and sincerely, upon obligations incurred by membership in these other groups. He finds himself in opposition to the autocratic commands of the superior when these commands would cause him to violate the rules, ethics, or procedures of the alternate institution. A professional social worker is not only an instrumentality of a social welfare agency but also a representative of a profession which imposes certain obligations which he may choose to honor. The person is not falsely pious in relating his actions to another allegiance, merely thoughtful. Any superior who forces a subordinate to violate the ethics or laws of another organization risks challenging more than the subordinate. She opens up the possibility that more powerful figures in the other organization or more powerful forms of influence from it will be activated. Most professional associations and unions develop a set of values which may be expressed in a code of ethics, a set of personal loyalties, possibly a social or political program or posture, and sometimes a strict definition of the nature of the rights and responsibilities in their work that is to be adopted by the members of the organization. Any or all of the assertions of principles, and the various institutional mechanisms for implementing the principles (e.g., ethics committees) may be utilized by the agent as he strives to combat authoritarianism.

There are two principal dangers to the agent when she relies upon structural supports to her position — the danger of moving over into rebellion and the danger of sliding downward into submission. On the one hand, by her behavior the subordinate continually threatens to provide a clash of a personal nature between herself and the superior. She moves along the edge of engaging in a rebellious struggle for primacy with the autocrat, a fight she can only lose and that can lead inexorably to expulsion from the system. On the other hand, when the agent begins by representing herself as dependent upon the structural supports, she may gradually come to see herself as passive and dependent and may tend to rely upon one or another support repetitively. Both in her passivity and her repetitive behavior, the agent may then tend to give up or ignore her duty to be an agent of struggle and change. Indeed, without choice, active diagnosis, tension between submission and rebellion, the person is no longer her own guide but sees herself instead as a mere tool subject to the control of others.

2. **The agent in countering authoritarianism needs to mobilize social supports to her position, supports neither coerced from others nor relied upon by the agent beyond their direct manifestations.**

The agent must concern himself with his peers, his own subordinates, and other superiors when he engages in struggle with autocratic elements of a superior's behavior. His focus in respect to social supports is different from his concern regarding structural supports. Rather than cast his dependency upon peers, subordinates or other superiors, the agent strives to activate tendencies present in these other persons that will be coordinated with his own anti-autocratic efforts. He must steer his way between dominating others and using them for his own purposes, or divesting himself of direct responsibility in carrying on the contest. His aim is to create equalitarianism in the organization by practicing it and demonstrating its potentials, and his accomplishment is hollow if it is not reached through mobilizing other people to also be agents of their own welfare.

I am familiar with this problem of mobilizing or activating the equalitarian dispositions of peers through my own series of somewhat dramatic failures in groups where the forces of authoritarianism and equalitarianism have confronted each other. Perhaps I can lean upon a description of the pattern in these failures to illustrate the content of a correct line of action.

The elements of the typical situation in which I acted wrongly are these:

> A person in authority is exercising his powers in a group of which I am a member. The person may be the chair of a department, head of an institution, leader of a prestigious committee, or acknowledged leader of a relatively informal group.
>
> The person is attempting to impose upon the group some policy or approach to group effort that is hierarchical in an authoritarian way. His purpose is to establish as an agreed-upon policy for the group a mode of operation that is autocratic and that leads to his benefit at the cost of the members of the group.
>
> To carry out his aim the leader must implicitly threaten the members of the group. He must communicate the notion that resistance to his proposals will be understood as an attack upon his rightful authority and any challenger will be subjected to some kind of punishment.
>
> Roused both by the autocratic nature of the proposal and the implied threat of harm, the members of the group are angry and fearful, wanting to contest the authority (i.e., rebellion) but also wanting to flee from the situation or resigning themselves to it (submitting). The members of the group are in a heightened state of tension and ambivalence toward the authority-figure, toward themselves, and toward their comrades.
>
> Past experience has shown the members of the group that they can be divided by the authority, isolated from each other, and that whichever member of the group is tagged as the person who represents the spirit of rebellion in the group will be especially singled out and hurt. There is a pervasive sense of vulnerability.
>
> Into this constellation of forces within a group I come, charged with excitement, exasperation, righteousness, indignation, with keen logic and power of character. I attack the proposal with clarity, but express my assault within the framework of profound feeling. I turn upon the person in authority with great vigor, but with such ferocity, sarcasm,

contempt or other manner of degradation that it seems to all observers that I am too personal, too angry, too involved in the combat to be at all reasonable.

I find to my dismay that I have unwittingly redirected the tension and ambivalence away from the authority and onto myself as object. I appear to my peers to be chastising them as well as the leader, to be looking down on them, to be trying to dominate them according to my will in just the way that the autocratic leader has been attempting to impose his proposition upon them. Those of my peers who might have fought the autocrat's moves tend to withdraw from the engagement lest they become rebellious like me, and they tend to become neutralized by their double ambivalence — that directed toward the superior and that directed toward me. I seem to chastise my peers because I probably do. I am exasperated because they have not acted more courageously or effectively, and I take on more of their responsibility and feeling that I have a right to assume.

The ambivalence of my peers toward the superior can be stated as follows. The superior is resented for his authoritarianism, but he is respected for his position of authority and whatever background led to attainment of that status as well as the power he can exert over them. The ambivalence of my peers toward me is: I am esteemed for diagnosing and resisting autocratic behavior, but disliked for being rebellious, for making my peers feel guilty about their submission, and for inhibiting their struggle to find their own ways of overcoming the unsuitability of the superior's proposal.

I can guess at some of the infantile determinants of this pattern that reflect my own ambivalence. Competition and identification with a severe and overwhelming father, sibling rivalry, a depressive disposition in which I must carry excessive responsibility in relationships and in which I must produce my own failures, are a few of the psychological issues involved. In other words, my failure in this example is a derivative of my own entrapment in authoritarianism. It consists of practices that move me into rebellion rather than into productive opposition. The error of rebellion arises in that I coerce not only the superior but also my peers; I dominate them, urge them to join my opposition beyond their own inclinations and readiness of the moment, or I am contemptuous of their faults or weaknesses as if I were superior to them. Fighting my own desires for passivity, I am overly critical when my peers appear to be passive. I am considerably more successful in opposing authoritarian acts when I am less ambivalent myself because then I am able to join together an attack upon the deficiencies of the autocratic proposition as well as activation of those among my peers who are also interested in creating increased equalitarianism.

Whem peers do become activated, it is necessary for the agent to coordinate herself with them in opposing autocratic behavior without becoming dependent upon them. In tough situations there comes to each of us the wish for passivity, once our comrades are aroused, the temptation born of the desire to be rescued from contradictory and intolerable troubles. We relax our guard, we admire the spirit and talent of our allies, we are relieved that we are not alone, and we slip ever so subtly into a spectator's role. Or we are distressed that our peers who speak out do so in ways that we do not approve, are halting and ineffective, are embarrassing, or perhaps rebellious, and as a consequence we fall silent, withdraw or disengage rather than cooperate despite difference.

We need not support all that our peers do to align ourselves with them in moments of action, indeed, such complete support would approach dependency. Rather, each of us, each individual, must retain the autonomy to choose and discriminate at the same time he works with others. When increasing pressures are brought by the autocrat, and those peers who have been activated or almost drawn into opposition face division and are threatened by the fracture of whatever unities have been developed, each person as agent will be called upon to regulate and coordinate himself, his peers and the authority so that neither rebellion nor submission wins the day.

When an agent tries to mobilize the social support of a superior other than the autocratic leader she is opposing, she needs to follow the same theme of activating without coercing or depending upon that other superior. The most natural inclination is to adopt the dependent posture, to seek a more benevolent superior who will outrank or outwit the oppressive individual. If a subordinate can find an alternate superior to carry out the negation of authoritarianism, she can remain passive and protected. With authority then allocated to the supposedly more benevolent superior, the oppressed subordinate need not stand forth as an autonomous figure.

This process of adopting the dependent posture, of course, is itself of an authoritarian nature. The subordinate does not assume the responsibility which should be appropriately hers in the equalitarian system that she desires. She leaves intact the definitions of initiative and accountability that have been asserted by the autocratic superior when she fails to bear her part as an agent. Even more, however, she affirms these definitions by her dependent reliance upon another superior. Whereas it may be appropriate to equalitarianism for a subordinate to ask a second superior to help a first abide by commonly accepted divisions of responsibility, it is authoritarian for a subordinate to dependently allow any superior to autonomously define the authority patterns.

Some of the issues common to the search for a benevolent superior were evident in the college library staff as they related to the autocratic head librarian. No working day passed without a full complement of her personal whims: one person must drive her to lunch, another must agree with her denunciation of her enemies, a third must in full abasement be reprimanded for no obvious reason at all. Members of the staff lived in dread that tomorrow they would be the object of her wrath and injustice. They lived as well in guilt that somehow they were being participants in the personal damnation and destruction of their peers because they themselves were afraid to contradict the boss. Morale was low, turnover of staff rapid, and the incidence of jagged nerves and psychosomatic disturbances quite high. Every week brought with it a new proposal by a member of the staff that was directed at appealing in some way to the librarian's overseers, either the vice-president of the institution, the president, the board of directors or an official of the state administration. Sometimes the thought was that a group of the staff would invoke this intervention, sometimes it was that a person who was secure, such as someone with tenure, should do so; sometimes it was that one of the individuals resigning from the library staff should carry out the onerous chore. Whatever the mode, the intention was consistent; the staff would throw themselves on the mercy of the superior's superior, thereby seeking rescue through dependency on the new authority.

If the head librarian had been an anomaly in the college, this wish would indeed have been realistic and equalitarian as well. Such would have been the case if the librarian had been far more authoritarian than the system in which she operated. She would have been violating the norms of the institution and would have been vulnerable to her superior who would have brought those norms to bear upon her performance. The staff members would then have been mobilizing the librarian's superior by being sources of information to him and nothing more. They would have been providers of the knowledge that the principles of organization of the school were being undermined. However, they would not have sought to coerce this librarian's boss nor would they have cast their dependency on him beyond expecting him to carry out the stated policies of the college.

If the librarian had been representative of the typical way in which authority was expressed in the college, the subordinates could not have realistically hoped to activate her superior as a means toward equalitarianism. If other departments and sections of the college were similarly oppressive and anti-democratic, and if the president were much like the librarian and in agreement with her, staff members would have found the president sympathetic to the librarian rather than to them. If there had been a pervasive quality of authoritarianism in the institution, the wish to invoke higher authority could have been nothing other than the helpless, unrealistic hope to be saved from evil, itself a form of authoritarian submission.

With superiors as with peers, therefore, the agent who aims to transform authoritarian into equalitarian hierarchies must act to mobilize social supports without forcing the support and without depending upon it beyond its open, momentary expression. The same principle holds true when an agent deals with persons subordinate to herself in the hierarchy at the same time she is contending with some autocratic endeavors of her superior. The agent in her role as superior must mobilize her subordinates without exploiting them or encouraging their dependency; she must awaken and foster their dispositions toward equalitarianism without pressing them to hold equalitarian positions in which they do not believe.

The twin dangers of dominating subordinates, that is, forcing them to comply with our rebellion, or leaning too heavily upon them to carry our own load in the anti-autocratic effort, occur repeatedly in our practical lives when we are in the role of superiors in organizations. When we dominate and avoid our responsibilities as agents, we take on the role of oppressor and hurt others as well as ourselves. The matter is further complicated. If we fail to mobilize our subordinates toward equalitarian participation, we implicitly acquiesce in the authoritarian status quo. If I am right that all or most of our social institutions are actually authoritarian, then there is much to be done in this arena of using our positions to activate our subordinates when we are in a higher role in a particular hierarchy. There is a narrow line between mobilizing subordinates and dominating them, a line that we rightfully fear to cross. But look at our alternative. If we neglect our duty to further equalitarianism within the authoritarian institutions of which we are a part, if in fear of being rebellious toward our superiors or dominating toward our subordinates, we prevent ourselves from developing social movement, then we are not innocent. Rather, we are in that manner instruments of authoritarianism.

Social workers face this matter often in therapeutic work with clients. Consider this example that students brought into class discussion one bright, sunny, spring day. A twelve-year-old boy was having difficulty with school adjustment (as they call it) and the clinical social worker was trying to have him accommodate to the school to relieve himself of pressure from that source. I put the following question to class, "Should the social worker encourage the boy to be submissive in respect to the demands of that school, or should the social worker rather help the boy contend socially and politically with the school?" It is not assuming in this question that the boy is all democratic and the school all autocratic. That would be highly unlikely. Rather, the question was asked to challenge the student social worker to examine whether he had (1) failed to mobilize the equalitarian components of the boy's dealings, (2) assumed and sided with the power and principles of organization of the school, and (3) thereby unwittingly dominated the boy and forced him to submit to the unjust as well as the proper authority of the school.

"But wait," insisted members of the class who were upset with the question. "If you encourage the boy to tangle with the school, you do him a disservice. On the one hand, you put him in an impossible position because he will lose in his contest with the school; on the other hand, you are unethical because you induce him to carry out your own antagonism toward the school system. You have made him a tool of your own values and your politics."

In answer to the second complaint, I replied that I would not coerce the boy's struggle against the school. At most, I would follow it when it arose — as it did for the social worker or we would not have been discussing it — or I would support that impulse to contention if it were strong within the psychological field of the boy. In other words, my effort would be directed at coordinating my involvement with the boy's endeavors and thus I would avoid being his dominator. Remember that if I were to ignore his disposition for struggle or try to negate it, I would not be innocent. In answer to the first charge leveled by the class, I suggested that we could not pre-judge whether the school was intractable, whether it was purely autocratic, or immune to our influence. Whatever the child's success with school authorities, indeed, even in the face of failure there, he would have gained greatly by the very presence of our cooperative involvement with him in a task of much salience in his life.

I was not proposing that the boy should fight alone, but that the social worker should extend and align himself alongside the actions of his client. He might support the boy's explorations of ways to contend with the school creatively or offer understanding of the behaviors that the youth had created and that had landed him in trouble. There are many ways that clinical social workers know to connect with people without approving the exact behaviors that they have exhibited. The social worker had no more right to depend upon the boy solving the problem alone, however, than he had the right to make the boy fight the social worker's battle. Indeed, part of the reason social workers have often not encouraged clients to fight authoritarianism in social settings in which they have no leverage is self-protection. Social workers themselves are persons who do not know how to oppose and survive effectively in their own agencies, yet they face the matter often in therapeutic work with clients, and know well that it is not easy to be an agent in countering authoritarianism by mobilizing social supports. Workers and clients can explore possibilities as equals and can learn from each other.

3. The agent who opposes authoritarianism circumvents, deflects or deflates struggles for personal superiority.

When a person becomes an agent in transforming an authoritarian situation, she is rapidly put in the presence of all manner of assaults of a personal nature. Because she acts independently of the existing principle of organization of the institution, the agent has injected a special note of personal assertion into the institution's life. In the nature of authoritarianism, such assertion is regarded by those who adhere to the autocratic principle to be the demonstration of a desire for personal superiority. The authoritarian system is built around permission bestowed upon the superior to dominate the subordinate, to generalize from functional authority to personal superiority. When a subordinate fails to accept her domination, she is perceived as wishing to oppress in her own right, abiding by the principle of dominate or be dominated. Working from the assumption that all social life entails a struggle for such personal domination, the autocratic superior thus believes his personality is challenged; he fails to realize that the assertion by the subordinate is directed at the institution's principles. As a result, the superior acts to defend his position and his person which are indistinct from each other in the superior's mind.

The endeavors of superiors to demonstrate and promote their personal superiority become a major battleground in the alteration of authoritarian into equalitarian systems. But the only victories in this highly charged arena come from transactions between superior and subordinate in which personal antagonisms are changed into mutual understanding of the faulty nature of the system within which they both exist. The superior insists upon open recognition and submission to his primacy in encounters, a primacy clearly divorced from and set above his answerability to the subordinate; or the superior increases the demands for excessive answerability from the subordinate. In either case, he uses a position in the hierarchy as a controlling weapon beyond anything that is appropriate to the tasks of the organization or to productive social transactions. It is straightforward authoritarianism within the hierarchical system when the superior acts as if such pressures and demands are tied to the work and tasks of the organization when, in fact, they pertain to his own need for self-aggrandizement.

In social work education we have an expression of a typical variation of this technique which involves a direct assault upon the agent-subordinate's personality and which illustrates well my point. A student who questions the wisdom of his supervisor or of a senior professional in an agency is confronted with the diagnosis that "he has problems with authority." (or he is too aggressive, impatient, idealistic, or rude.) It is expected that when the student is given this picture of himself, he should search his soul and find the root for the inappropriateness in personal weaknesses, whereupon he can correct these defects and adjust more realistically to the requirements or orders placed upon him. It is often recommended on these grounds alone that the student needs personal therapy or is in the wrong profession.

Now it is perfectly true that frequently students do have problems with authority in the sense that they are excessively rebellious or submissive for reasons that derive from past experiences with parents, teachers and other authorities. We could not expect otherwise given the degree of authoritarianism throughout our society that fosters distortions in human relations. It is similarly true that students, like all of us, need to examine over and over again their own part in troublesome social relationships. What makes the supervisor's diagnosis of the student's problem a carrier of personal domination — in those instances when it serves as domination rather than as a realistic, pertinent and helpful observation — is the inequality in answerability that accompanies it. The student is held to account for the difficulties that have arisen, but the authority is not made equally answerable, nor is the whole system of allocation of authority examined with reference to the specific issue. In an analysis which directs excessive accountability upon the student, the subordinate in this transaction, a propriety and correctness on the part of the superior is implied along with the assumption of impropriety and incorrectness on the part of the student.

A comparable example comes from a friend of mine who was in the midst of psychotherapy at the same time she was differing with her boss on some professional decisions he had made. This chief frequently referred to the personality problems of my friend as factors that intruded upon her good judgment, focusing upon these problems especially when he wanted her to agree to support decisions he had reached unilaterally. By this means he provoked in my friend all the defensiveness, diffidence, outrage, resentment, distress and helplessness that customarily accompany any forced submission to personal domination. Apart from the fact that her therapy probably increased the soundness of her judgment, the boss's reliance upon the personal part of the subordinate's life while preventing her from similarly centering upon his particular personality problems was of crucial significance in defining the act as autocratic.

The tendency of students, of my friend, and most of us in such situations is to become ensnared in the web of submission and rebellion, or else to alternate submission in the presence of authorities with rebellion in the presence of peers. The thrust of the personal attack is such that failure to submit to the analysis rendered by the superior is considered by the superior as rebellion and as proof that there exists a problem with authority; and failure to rebel against the unjust diagnosis is debasing in the subordinate's own eyes. With great bitterness, the subordinate resorts to defensive, self-righteous pronouncements. The superior becomes a personal enemy.

The solution for the subordinate is to diminish both the excessive submission and the excessive rebellion so that he opposes yet survives. The subordinate must bring about a balance between appropriate self-criticism and self-discovery on the one side, and pertinent criticism and evaluation of the authority and the institution, on the other. For instance, a given agent would be sincerely willing to explore the idea that he might have problems with authority, and begin to examine that possibility in analysing and reviewing events that have occurred. As the examination proceeded, however, he would also necessarily direct attention to the behavior of the superior. By this means, he would be accepting the primacy of the superior in setting the possibility of his personal fault without necessarily accepting the truth of the charge ("I may have this trouble, let us look to see if it is truly the case."), and this receptivity might prevent a contest over who has primacy in the relations. Further, the agent could acknowledge the reality of whatever distortion he brings to the superior-subordinate relation, but he would also be careful to invoke critical analysis of others involved in the situation. Only if this last point is brought out successfully can the effort at personal domination be transformed into mutual exploration of reality.

There are many avenues to the solution other than that which I have sketched out above. The common theme in all of them, I think, is that they neutralize the hierarchical component that rests upon personal inferiority, turning the line of inquiry from concentration upon personal deficiencies of the subordinate to study of the personal problems of subordinate and superior as these are connected with inadequacies in the general system. The main accomplishment is the joining of personal limitations to the faults in the system, seeing their interconnectedness and the consequent necessity for mutual support and common effort in the face of problems and contradictions the system imposes upon both of them.

It is vital that the subordinate not fall into the trap of attacking the personality of the superior in defending herself against the charges to which she is held answerable. When one is demeaned, it is natural to reply in kind. But to answer personal affront with personal affront is to transfer the hierarchical difference to the personal sphere entirely and to foster personal superiority strivings by the autocrat. The agent must direct her attention principally to the bias of the institution. Preoccupation with the faults of the superior seen separately from the institutional context distracts from that emphasis when the agent is defending her personal integrity.

I have earlier suggested that the agent should try to diagnose the autocratic superior's style and personality for use in dealing with him in respect to structural and social supports. I am not contradicting that view here; rather, I am noting that an agent does not deflate tension over personal dominance by trying to equalize with the autocrat through analysis of the superior's personal deficiencies. The subordinate does not learn the personality of his superior so that he may degrade his attacker because he himself feels demeaned. An exchange of personal assaults only puts greater distance between the two and makes for more reliance upon arbitrary control by the superior. The long-range goal of enlisting all persons in the system in the equalitarian effort is hindered rather than facilitated by power games. Few people are influenced to productive effort by attacks on the personality of a superior by an embattled, defensive subordinate since the superior can always justify the behavior as response to his position and as reflection of the subordinate's own inadequacies. Others in the system may recognize the truth of the subordinate's assessment yet they discount it in part because it stems from self-defense and they resent the subordinate for urging them into dangerous waters. The subordinate himself is unsatisfied because striking back at injustice does not change the overall hierarchical relations that permit the unfair encounter.

It is important that subordinates become aware of the fact that superiors are mere persons rather than the flawless and omnipotent figures which they often seem to be. In E.Y. Harburg's words, "No matter how high or great the throne, what sits on it is the same as your own."[4] I spelled out one reason for knowing the quirks of an autocratic superior when I referred to learning how to rely upon structural supports or active social supports in concrete social conditions. The more one understands as a subordinate, the more clever her maneuvering toward equalitarianism will be in these activities. For instance, if an agent can determine how far the superior's personal authoritarianism deviates from the authoritarianism common to the institution, she can be more certain when there are attempts to activate the superior's superior. The greater the disparity, the more probability there is of useful intervention stemming from higher levels of the hierarchy if information can be gotten through to the persons in these positions.

A second reason for expertly diagnosing superiors is to include knowledge of that person's character in the perception of the system itself. One does not fully understand an authoritarian system until he appreciates the oppression of all members of the system, and one element of that comprehension follows from viewing the superior and her problems in the context of her role in the institution. For no matter how impervious the superior may first appear to be to the same constraints under which the agent is in struggle, she is also subject to similar domination and limits.

Because the superior is also subjected to the constraints of the authoritarian system, she is necessarily ambivalent toward it. Central to any subordinate's diagnosis of his superior must be an understanding of the existence of this ambivalence and the way in which it is handled by the superior. Most of the time we perceive only one side of a superior's ambivalence, her antagonism to opposition and determination to maintain her own power. We come to believe falsely that superiors are single-minded and secure in their main purpose, in the very same way that we believe they are independent of the principles underpinning the institution. But it is inherently the case that superiors are ambivalent about authoritarian systems, precisely because they too are dominated by them. The apparent power and self-direction connected with being a superior are illusory, as we all know from our own sense of powerlessness when we are superiors but which we forget when we are subordinates.

A superior appears most forceful when she is implementing the authoritarianism of an authoritarian institution. All the means of the system facilitate her endeavors when she is acting in accord with the principle of organization of the system. But on some level, every superior knows that she can effectively register her own will, her unique contribution, her individuality only if it furthers that which already exists. If the superior tries to impose herself in ways that diverge from the accepted paths, her power dissipates rapidly. When she is different and special, when she is truly innovative, that person violates the constraining qualities of an authoritarian hierarchy, and the forces within that hierarchy, carried by subordinates as well as peers and superiors, are suddenly arrayed against her. She is viewed as being excessively self-serving and she discovers the conditional nature of her independent authority. The superior is made ambivalent with the authoritarian system by the demands upon her from that system to control and deny those parts of self which are most special.

Furthermore, an authoritarian organization produces ambivalence in every one of its members including the superior because it systematically separates a person from others and places him over against them. The person must be isolated from subordinates in order for his authority to be maintained; he is alone among functional equals because they are potential competitors; and he is kept apart from his own superiors by their need to protect their own autonomy and power. The loneliness with which the person must live turns the individual against himself as well.

If every superior in an authoritarian hierarchy is ambivalent toward the system and about his own place in that system, why is that fact noted so rarely? Why do most of us recognize only the positive attachment to their positions by superiors in autocracies? Where is the negative side of the ambivalence? I think there are two answers to these questions. When the negative side of the ambivalence does appear, when a superior exposes his antagonism to the authoritarian system, persons around him do not credit such an attitude as being significant. The superior is not clearly heard in the substance of his complaint, which is his dissatisfaction with the system. People assume that superiors are content in their roles despite evidence to the contrary. That is one answer, and there is a second one equally as important. It is most often the case that the superior himself does not clearly *experience* or *reveal* his ambivalence; he is intolerant of it and allows only positive regard into awareness. In short, the superior may be incapable of the conscious experience of ambiguity or ambivalence.

Thus, in diagnosis, subordinates can look for the degree to which the superior tolerates and shares ambivalence concerning the authoritarianism of the institution. The more her ambivalence is available to her and to those around, the more equalitarian in character is the superior; the more single-minded with respect to the system she seems to be, the more authoritarian she is. The degree of conscious, aware ambivalence in the character of the superior can be compared by the observant subordinate with the policies of the organization to see how typical or deviant the superior is from the norms that predominate. The superior with a more equalitarian personality structure will facilitate efforts to change the guiding principles of the institution and will be unlikely to engage in struggles of personal superiority. The person with the more authoritarian character, however, will show only opposition to those who are trying to change the principles, denying the underlying ambivalence which is present in him.

There is one point at which even the superior with the most authoritarian personality structure will become aware of his ambivalence, when his personal tendency to avoid consciousness of ambivalence will be overwhelmed by the social situation. That is the point at which the institution has been qualitatively changed into a more equalitarian system. When a successful transformation does take place, even the most autocratic individual seems finally to discover the negative components of the authoritarian organization and the positive traits of the equalitarian one.

The idea I am putting forth is that equalitarian relations, once achieved, prove to be as attractive to the dominator as to the subordinate figure. We ovelook this exactly to the degree that the superior is out of touch with his resentment of the authoritarian system, to the extent, that is, that he possesses an intolerance of ambivalence. In responding only to his conscious and apparent defense of the system, we are insensitive to a hidden potential support in the form of the superior's repressed dislike for the authoritarianism he supports openly.

There is a special type of personal domination that is fostered by a system which separates primacy and accountability, adding excessive primacy upwards in a hierarchy and extra accountability downwards. It is almost a pure or ideal type for authoritarian organizations, and it is overwhelming in its impact upon subordinates subjected to its effects. When we once talked together in a class about this type of domination, everyone who had ever been faced with it in the past became immediately almost as agitated and upset as each had been when he or she was originally under the influence of the superior who manifested this style. The impact is powerful not only in the short run but over long periods of time. Two main attributes underlie this type of personal domination. First, the person in a position of authority dispalys one aspect of what is known in psychoanalysis as an anal-erotic character trait. Ernest Jones points to the phenomenon in question in the following description:

"... the opposition displayed against any attempt from without to indicate conduct, and the resentment shown against any attempt to thwart conduct that has been decided on... The person objects equally to being made to do what he doesn't want to do, and to being prevented from doing what he wants to do..."[5]

A superior who operates from this stance, thus, expects his desires to be rendered exactly as he wants them by subordinates. Whatever contribution that comes up from a subordinate must become his own before it is viable. If the subordinate does not insure that suggested actions are identified as the superior's, he violates the superior and arouses his animosity because he is presumed to be trying to "indicate conduct" from without or "thwart conduct that has been decided on."

Second, the person in authority who manifests this type of personal domination is an individual who cannot tolerate intense emotional feelings within himself, but rather needs to experience them as coming from outside by arousing them in others. Rage and anxiety are the main emotions that such a person cannot possess within his own experience but must perceive in others. When such an individual is present in circumstances that threaten to make him angry or anxious, he does not allow himself to feel the rage or anxiety. The person is afraid to hold these emotions vividly because he expects to be overcome by them or to destroy others under their influence. Instead of experiencing his own feelings, such a person subtly provokes the emotions in subordinates, thereby finding a means to express and experience them.

Subordinates in these relationships have a very difficult time of it. They find themselves angry, but they do not know why they are angry or why they are as enraged as they have become. Their emotions are out of proportion to the apparent directives, commands, or other means by which they are being dominated. They are twice over angry, once in reaction to the arbitrary authority imposed upon them, and once for carrying the load of the superior's emotion. They are angry for themselves and for the superior, though they do not realize this and are further upset because they are confused and torn apart within. When they try to unravel the mess they are in, they find that they are contesting with the superior, which adds to their own anger and to that of the superior as well. A vicious cycle ensues which is sado-masochistic in nature.

The subordinate who is controlled by a superior whose character is structured along these lines finds herself faced with the ultimate in authoritarian control, the more so when the institution is thoroughly biased in the same direction. Her person is not her own, but is a means for another, even to the extreme that her feelings are also experienced as foreign. The subordinate learns further that the proposals for work that she generates must first be rejected, violently, personally rejected, by the superior since they are presumed to represent efforts toward becoming primary in the relationship. She then discovers that the very suggestions she has made which were once renounced, are later forced upon her as directives, but this time as the expressions of the superior's insights. The subordinate is expected to follow these directives absolutely and to discreetly avoid noticing that they were her own ideas in the first place, lest she be indicted as rebellious. The person has been molested by being robbed of her ideas or practices. Since neither her feelings nor her competencies can be her own, the individual is made empty by her circumstance, is divested of her integrity as a person, and is made inferior to another in a personal sense.

The pure type of authoritarian control produces the pure type of reaction — craven submission or agitated rebellion. Side by side will be found subordinates who accept the superior's tactics and identify with them, and subordinates who reject them entirely. Within each subordinate as well can be found the impulses toward submission and toward rebellion. Contempt of others vies with hatred of self, common fate with isolation, relief with profound helplessness. Since every aspect of life becomes personal in an unhappy way, the desire for impersonal living conditions wells up. Estrangement and alienation follow.

When this plight is in force, struggle in the immediate depends quite heavily upon activity directed to the long run. Agents must continue to probe in all ways in the direct encounters, but they also have to keep a close connection between present and future thrusts in order that they not be destroyed or ejected too easily. Reliance upon long-term institutional change cannot substitute for immediate contention, as I have said earlier, because the renunciation of direct counteraction too easily becomes submission; it can only be constructive to work on long-range projects if such effort contains direct and immediate actions that are significant to the agent.

VI

The practical domain of long-range contesting with authoritarianism is immense. It includes community organization, union development, legal and legislative proceedings, creation of voluntary groupings, grievance procedures within institutions and other exertions that can be seen as building the necessary structural and social supports for those who risk in the name of equalitarianism. Rather than pretend to more than I possess, and reluctant to push my conceptions too far beyond my practical experience, I will restrict myself to limited commentary.

In promoting structural supports for those who try to transform authoritarian institutions, it is basic for each actor to connect mutually with persons who are most in touch with immediate transactions regarding arbitrary authority. A lawyer may have great expertise in the ways of the courts, a social worker may know the realm of social and welfare services, the educator may know his school system; but if these experts are not jointly dependent with others who are also counteracting autocratic leadership, they inevitably align themselves within the principles of organization of the institutions surrounding them. No individual, however, competent and equalitarian in style as she may be, is capable of single-handedly mastering system principles without being held answerable and accountable. The necessary question that follows is, answerable to whom? Acceptance of any sort of credential as proof of obligation or accountability obscures the vision of the expert because credentials are linked to the past (whether rendered effective by professional schools, the licensing practices of the state, or by one's comrades in struggles from the past) and derive from forces that are dead, slightly operative or already in the service of established authoritarian hierarchies. To be divorced from open, alive accountability to those engaged in direct, immediate challenges against autocracy is to be primary without the necessary answerability that assures equality, thus to be oneself inclined toward authoritarianism.

What applies to "experts" in dealing with rules, policies, laws, mass organizations, etc., pertains equally to those persons who exist in the rank and file and who are developing structural supports toward equalitarianism. The proper answerability-primacy relation can hold only when both facets of responsibility (responsibility to others, responsibility for initiatives) are concurrently active and related to the people and the groups shouldering the equalitarian load. As every union member knows, the union leader cannot be too separated from the time, geography and dynamics of daily work without himself becoming authoritarian. So, too, every activist is aware that leaders who defend poor and outspoken clients tend to become masters rather than collaborators unless bound to the hurts and risks of oppression and resistance. Any position, prestige or competence that provides a person with consistent initiative must always be balanced by equally consistent accountability to those who allow the primacy, and an agent is successful only to the extent he is tied intimately to those collaborating in the system change.

Agents who direct their main activity toward mobilizing others to participate cooperatively in transforming authoritarian institutions must master a set of problems among these others that come from the fears, distrust, uncertainty and defensiveness that are natural adaptations to oppression. The aim of such agents is essentially that of creating the conditions and means whereby all persons in an institution are repeatedly changing all others through their transactions. Creating equalitarian practices within the authoritarian system to the point where such practices deny the realization of authoritarianism means enabling each person to transform himself as well as others so that the self-oppression and services to the oppressive system are rooted out in fact. The accomplishment of this goal depends upon finding ways to recognize and negate the authoritarian components of each member's behavior and to recognize and facilitate the equalitarian components to be found in each member too.

To mobilize oppressed people is arduous and frustrating. Impatient, endowed with a sense of crisis, agents commonly try to coerce allegiance to their movement. I have seen this many times in leftist circles and have been put off by it. The agent represents himself or his group as having an understanding of the problems of all oppressed and a solution to these problems. He implies that what is needed is only the support, the following, the disciplined obedience of the persons who are oppressed, and once he is provided with that backing, his group will lead the way.

Persons who stand for this vanguard perspective are usually anti-psychological and interpret all concerns for the inner life and problems of the oppressed as reactionary. In political discussions they generally react to any suggestion of psychological implications with contempt and annoyance. They consider it diversionary and frivolous to attend to the feelings of political activists. Sometimes it is projected that any attention to psychodynamics or group dynamics is merely displaced psychotherapy, self-indulgence or excessive preoccupation with group process at the expense of collective achievement. Their opposition to the psychological component of social action is very intense, and they are usually successful in intimidating or driving away persons who are sensitive to such matters.

A more subdued version of this coercive method — this method which arrogates initiative to the vanguard, loyalty to the followers —

occurs in occupational, educational and other social institutions. Those who stand out against the authoritarian leader in open challenge and who concurrently dominate their colleagues, want the backing of these comrades at a later time and for the long haul. They usually justify the correctness of their actions in the past confrontation without adequate self-criticism. When this unqualified support is not forthcoming, these self-appointed leaders condemn the character and morality of their colleagues; they imply that their initiative, however faulty, should have been accepted.

The distortion through which this destructive drama unfolds seems to be as follows. Great emphasis is placed by the actor upon the evils of the offending autocratic leader, the ruling class, or some personification of the authoritarian system. That we all contribute to the development and implementation of the authoritarian system, that we all support as well as suffer from it, is obscured or denied. The ruling class or leader is pictured as very powerful and singularly bad; the followers are weak and good. Those in the middle who do not loudly denounce the rulers or leaders are their servants. The key to this approach is excessive blame upwards and lack of respect for the contradictoriness that brings the oppressed to cause their own pain while they cry out against it.

To counteract this distortion it is imperative to be realistic in analysis. Part of the long-term job for an agent who wishes to mobilize social support is to make a diagnostic assessment of the autocrat and to share that assessment with as many persons as can be brought together. Such appraisals must dignify the autocrat by recognizing his or her humanness and particularity, as well as demystify him or her by discerning how the superior is buffetted by personality problems and by the system's principles of operation. It is very easy to omit the dignifying parts in the midst of the wrath and pain generated by such autocratic figures, but depersonalizing them threatens one's compatriots. An agent who fails to bring into his comprehension the humanity of his enemy seems to be emulating that very enemy in his practice of dehumanization. Observers who may share the antagonism toward an autocratic leader shy away from agents who ask them to place all the unmitigated blame on the shoulders of the leader because they know intuitively that such allocation is untruthful; it avoids their own contribution to their oppression.

In addition to a realistic assessment of the autocrat, the agent needs to bring into play criticism of himself and of all participants in the short-term conflicts with arbitrary authority. No such conflict proceeds without error, poor judgment, faulty timing, extra pushing and too soon withdrawing, factors arising from the authoritarianism and the psychological deformations among us all. The dissection of these mistakes serves several purposes: it reveals the involvement of each person in the negatives of the organization, not merely as victim but as actor, and it thereby educates about reality; it suggests the potential power of members; it inhibits placing too much blame on a leader; it is the practice of mutuality and equality that leads to greater facility in functioning reciprocally and equitably; and it suggests ways of correcting wrong methods of confrontation.

One quite commonplace event is a good place to begin such an analysis, according to my experience. After an arbitrary authority has successfully imposed his domination, the persons affected often come together to commiserate with each other. They express their rage, frustration, hurt and helplessness and support one another in damning the leader and covering over their own weaknesses. Sometimes they even vow to work together — next time. But when next time comes along, they repeat the process: submission in the moment that authority is wielded, rebellion in the privacy of the aftermath. This is a kind of self-indulgence and mutual forgiveness that prolongs the subjection rather than counters it. During these gripe sessions, were mutual criticism and self-criticism instituted, much of the guilt and anxiety would have become explicit, and, being shared, it would be available to be mastered. I have found that I trust people who do not allow me to shift my part in my own defeat onto my opponents and who challenge me clearly in just these kinds of sessions.

A variant of this process is vividly presented by George Jackson in "From Dachau, Soledad Prison, California," although his version is incomplete in that it contains submission without the solution.

"I've seen the 'keeper' slap a man at the food serving line, take his tray and send him back to his cell without dinner. The man that was slapped may have been old enough to be the 'keeper's' father. The urge to strike out at the 'keeper' will almost always be repressed. In fact, most of the spontaneous fistfights between inmates occur immediately following an encounter between one of the participants of the fight and a 'keeper.'"[6]

Jackson improperly attributes cowardice to these inmates who repress their hatred of the guards and attack their peers, but in his writing he surpasses his contempt and develops compassion as he begins to understand why they behave as they do. His insight that the repressed hatred toward the keeper was released upon fellow inmates would have been most useful during the fighting itself because it would have fostered comprehension by the inmates of their feelings and impulses when the self-hatred and contempt of each other were most intense. The fighting among the inmates, like the commiseration among dominated persons when the authority is safely distant, is a contribution to authoritarianism rather than a challenge to it. Common interpretation of this fact and mutual support in the presence of it constitute equalitarian responses to a most painful circumstance.

VII

One disclaimer requires to be presented before I close this essay. Some persons may think that the tone of this esay is too hopeful and that I have not captured adequately the apathy, dismay, mistrust and other emotions that result from the struggle of moving from oppression to equality and cooperative support. The impression may have been given that transforming authoritarian organizations into equalitarian ones is possible without too much trouble. I do not believe this for a moment. My own experience has taught me that social change is difficult to carry out. It is full of pain, failure, set-backs, as well as just plain drudgery.

I have been trying to specify, however, what appear to me to be some social-psychological ingredients for what amounts to revolutionary actions. Only when the whole world of people are changing themselves, at the same time they are influencing others, can equalitarianism be approached. I have written, as I would like to live, in the spirit of William Morris' remarkable words:

"... and how men fight and lose the battle, and the thing they fought for comes about in spite of their defeat, and when it comes turns out not to be what they meant, and other men have to fight for what they meant under another name...."[7]

and those of Lu Hsun:

"I thought: hope cannot be said to exist, nor can it be said not to exist. It is just like roads across the earth. For actually the earth had no roads to begin with, but when many men pass one way, a road is made."[8]

Notes

1. Conceptually, the intention to accommodate to oppression by inhibiting one's efforts at combatting it represents the approach of fundamentalist religion. The aim is to empty the present, because it is painful and seems to be beyond the scope of effective self-assertion, hoping thereby that the future will provide greater reward. If present temptations are overcome, one will be rewarded in the afterlife for one's virtue. This basic tenet of religion, the bland present and rewarding future, has a counterpart in the social sciences in the concept that links maturity with the ability to delay gratification. It is argued that mature persons are able to withstand immediate gains in the interest of later fulfillment. According to this interpretation, self-denial in the present is a sign that one has merely recognized the demands of reality and adjusted to them appropriately.

2. Che Guevara. *Guerrilla Warfare.* New York: Monthly Review Press, 1961.

3. "Here the patient broke off, got up from the sofa, and begged me to spare him the recital of the details. I assured him that I myself had no taste whatever for cruelty, and certainly had no desire to torment him, but that naturally I could not grant him something which was beyond my power. He might just as well ask me to give him the moon. The overcoming of resistances was a law of treatment, and on no consideration could it be dispensed with." Sigmund Freud. "Notes Upon a Case of Obsessional Neurosis." In: *The Complete Psychological Works of Sigmund Freud, Volume X,* James Strachey, Senior Editor. London: Hogarth, 1955.

4. E.Y. Harburg. *Rhymes for the Irreverent.* New York: Grossman, 1965.

5. Ernest Jones. "Anal Erotic Character Traits." In: *Papers on Psycho-Analysis.* Boston: Beacon, 1961.

6. George Jackson. *Soledad Brother: The Prison Letters of George Jackson.* New York: Bantam, 1970.

7. William Morris. *A Dream of John Ball.* In *William Morris: Selected Writings,* G.D.H. Cole, Editor. New York: Random House, 1948.

8. Lu Hsun. *Chosen Pages of Lu Hsun.* New York: Cameron Associates, n.d.

INDEX

Abraham, Karl, 57

Accountibility, 34, 61–64, 66–68, 71–75, 91, 95, 99

Activists, 59, 102

Adorno, T. W., 57

Agent, 61, 84-104

Agitation, 3, 10-12, 17, 18, 20

Aiken, Conrad, 43-44, 57

Alcoholics, 12, 27-28, 55

Alive, 3-4, 15-29

Altruistic, 26-27

Ambivalence, 37, 41, 70, 89-90, 98
 intolerance of, 47, 51, 57, 98-99
 of superiors, 97-99

Anal-erotic character trait, 99

Anger, 41, 78-80, 89-90, 100

Angyal, Andras, 29, 45, 57

Answerability, 63-64, 66-75, 94-95
 excessive, 64, 67, 73, 74
 lesser, 71-72

Answerable, 62-66, 96, 101-102

Anti-psychological, 102

Anticipation, 46, 51, 53
 essential ambivalent, 45-57
 of the future, 44

Anxiety, 12, 46, 100, 104

Apathy, 3, 104

Arousal, 4, 17

Artistic inspiration, 28

Asian-American, 40

Athletic, 16, 28

Attitude, 7, 44, 57

Authoritarian, 3-4, 34, 38-39, 46-49, 59, 79, 98, 102-103
 authority, 6, 12-13, 23, 38, 60, 78, 89
 institutions, 3, 35, 41, 63-64, 66-68, 71, 77, 84, 93, 97, 99-100
 leadership, 9, 70, 101-103
 organizations, 15, 59, 66, 68-69, 70, 77
 personality, 64, 99
 principle, 45-46, 87

Authoritarianism, 3-6, 40, 57, 59-60, 63, 70-71, 81-83, 89-90, 92, 94-99, 101, 104

Authoritative, 6, 45

Authority, 6, 22, 34-35, 38, 45-46, 57, 60, 67, 69, 70, 79-80, 93, 96, 99
 arbitrary, 24, 59-60, 85, 100, 101, 103
 authoritarian, 6, 13, 23, 38, 60, 78, 89
 benevolent, 60
 equalitarian, 6, 13, 23-24, 34, 38
 laissez-faire, 13
 problems with, 23, 89-90, 95-96

Autocratic, 60, 71, 81, 87, 91, 103
 rule, 3

Automation, 48

Autonomy, 19-22, 64-65, 67, 72, 79, 84, 91, 98
 pseudo –, 65

Awe, 15-16

Balance of self-assertion and mergence striving, 19-20, 24-27
 of primacy and accountability, 62, 64, 66-68, 70, 102

Balint, Michael, 57

Basic trust, 57

Benedek, Therese, 45, 57

Bernard, L. Diane, 76

Bias, 48, 52-54, 82 96, 100

Blacks, 40-41

Blau, Deborah, 16, 25

Board, Cynthia, 29

Boss, 5, 60, 91, 95

Braverman, Harry, 35, 42

Breuer, Josef, 29

Bridgman, Percy, 4

Bureaucrats, 60, 72-73

Burgers, J.M., 46, 57

Burke, Kenneth, 65, 76

Capital punishment, 53-54

Capitalistic society, 41

Carla, 16, 25

Caseworkers, 2, 21-22, 60, 62-63, 66-67, 69-71

Character disorders, 55

Child psychiatry clinic, 36, 51, 60

Child-parent relations, 5, 20, 45-46, 95